"The brilliance of this book is that it relieves two tensions with each other. It gives detail to the otherwise ethereal while bringing nearness to the otherwise distant. Many of us talk 'union with Christ' in such vague ways, while viewing the contours of Jesus' own life from afar. But Brian Hedges seeks to remedy both troubles in one fell swoop. As we press our union with Jesus into the whole of his life, the doctrine becomes real, and the stories come to life. We see, and feel, with freshness that the one to whom we're joined by faith truly is for us, from Bethlehem to Baptism to Golgotha to Glory."

–**David Mathis**, Executive Editor, desiringGod.org;
Pastor, Cities Church, Minneapolis, MN; author, *Habits of Grace: Enjoying Jesus through the Spiritual Disciplines*

"When we think about the Christian life as union with Christ, we often turn to Paul's letters where the doctrine is explained so clearly. But this book equips us to go one step further in: To take up the story of Jesus itself and find our salvation in each of the major moments of the Gospels. So richly traditional that it may strike some readers as novel, Brian Hedges' new book is an invitation to a profound encounter with the saving life of Christ."

—**Fred Sanders,** Professor of Theology, Torrey Honors Institute,
Biola University, CA; Author, *The Deep Things of God: How the Trinity Changes Everything*

"This book may change the way you study the life of Christ. It will help you to read the gospels, not as a bystander watching the events occur, but as a participant because of our union with Christ. God the Son took on my nature and was born as a man, identified with me as a sinner in his baptism, fought for me in his temptations, and displayed his glory to me on the mountain. He prepared to drink down the wrath of God for me in the garden, though innocent he stood condemned for me at his trials, then he both died and rose again for my salvation, and I died and rose again with him. More than that, he ascended in his glorified human nature and I am seated with him in the heavenly places. One day soon, when Christ returns, I will appear with him in glory! Read this and you will see how you too can find your place in story of Jesus."

—**Allan Kenitz,** Pastor, Reformed Baptist Church, Kalamazoo, MI

"Union with Christ is a vital doctrine for the Christian life (in more than one sense). The church has been well served by excellent systematic theological treatments of the doctrine. But this book does something more profound. Hedges here wanders the pages of the New Testament gospels with the reader, showing us union with Christ. He takes the abstract and makes it concrete. He renders the concrete with a profoundly biblical stroke. And the result is not only concrete and biblical, but an essentially personal portrait of life in Christ. This is a thrilling read: Christ-soaked, gospel-saturated, well written, and broadly informed (the sidebars throughout are a wonderful addition). Hedges doesn't want to leave a single stone of the glory of Jesus' life unturned – and he doesn't want us to miss a single drop of the life-giving water we can drink as we come to him, hear his voice, and walk in his steps. Hugh Martin's theological acuity and pastoral heart have here found a twenty-first century voice."

—**Luke Potter,** Pastor, New City Presbyterian Church, South Bend, IN

"While the theme of the believer's union with Christ is woven throughout the New Testament, far too many Christians are unaware of its meaning or application. Oh, what they are missing! Once again, my friend Brian Hedges has written a biblically sound book that is rich with doctrine, church history, Puritan authors and even a reference to *Lord of the Rings*. Plus, he writes as a pastor with practical living woven throughout. This book has depth and accessibility—a perfect combination for exploring such a critical theme like union with Christ."

—**Mark Vroegop,** Pastor, College Park Church, Indianapolis, IN

"Brian Hedges is one of my favorite contemporary Christian authors. In this current volume, he brings the depth of the Puritans to our understanding of union with Christ. This book engages us in a fresh and compelling discussion of being with Jesus in all the stages of his work as our Savior. Get it. Read it. Savor what it means to be *With Jesus*."

—**Tedd Tripp**, Pastor, Author, International Conference Speaker

WITH JESUS

Finding Your Place in the Story of Christ

BRIAN G. HEDGES

With Jesus: *Finding Your Place in the Story of Christ*
© 2017 by Brian G. Hedges

ISBN:
Print: 978-1-63342-106-6
Mobi: 978-1-63342-124-0
ePub: 978-1-63342-113-4

Published by **Shepherd Press**
P.O. Box 24
Wapwallopen,
Pennsylvania 18660

eBooks: www.shepherdpress.com/ebooks

BP 24 23 22 21 20 19 18 17
    13 12 11 10   9   8   7   6   5   4   3   2   1

Library of Congress Cataloging-in-Publication Data
Names: Hedges, Brian G., author.
Title: With Jesus : finding your place in the story of Christ / Brian G. Hedges.
Description: Wapwallopen : Shepherd Press Inc., 2017. | Includes bibliographical references.
Identifiers: LCCN 2017049712 | ISBN 9781633421066 (pbk. : alk. paper) | ISBN 9781633421134
    (epub ebook)
Subjects: LCSH: Jesus Christ--Biography. | Identity (Psychology)--Religious aspects Christianity.
Classification: LCC BT301.3.H43 2017 | DDC 232--dc23 LC record available at
    https://lccn.loc.gov/2017049712

Cover Design by Content & Communication
Typesetting by www.**documen**.co.uk
Printed in the United States of America

To Holly

Contents

The Scriptures in explaining the scheme of redemption make frequent use of expressions of this general form: "Christ for us." "He was made sin for us." "He was made a curse for us." "He gave himself for us." "He gave himself a ransom for many." He is set forth manifestly crucified for us. He died for us. He appeareth in the presence of God for us. These, and many other similar expressions, are grounded on the fact that, according to the counsels of the everlasting covenant, Jesus was by the Father appointed, and of his own free and joyful will became, our Surety, our Representative. The scheme of redemption is founded on a marvelous exchange of places between Christ and his people, he taking theirs, they being translated into his....

[The] Scriptures in asserting our actual participation in this redemption, make frequent use of expressions of this other general form: "We with Christ." "We are crucified with Christ." "We are dead with him." "We are buried with him." "We are quickened together with him." "We are raised up together with him." "We are risen with Christ." "We are made to sit with him in heavenly places." In fact every expression of the form "Christ for us" may be regarded as having its corresponding relative expression, "We with him."

Hugh Martin[1]

Introduction

Therefore, if anyone is in Christ, he is a new creation. The old has
passed away; behold, the new has come.

2 Corinthians 5:17

Sam and Frodo stand on the brink of Mordor. They have embarked
on a dangerous quest: to destroy the Ring of Power. Pondering the
ancient legends of Middle Earth, Sam says, "I wonder what sort of a
tale we've fallen into?"[1]

Have you ever thought this about your life? Have you ever
wondered what kind of tale you've fallen into? Have you ever ques-
tioned what kind of story you are living?

You may look at your life, and think, "This is an interesting story,
but I have no idea where it's headed." Or, "This story is painful. I hope
there's a happy ending." Or maybe, "I'm bored. Can I trade stories
with someone else?"

Whatever the shape of your life, whether your personal saga is
comedy, tragedy, adventure, or soap opera, the gospel resounds with

good news for all who believe: *you've been inserted into a new story—the story of Christ.*

This book is about finding your place in the story of Jesus.

Reading the Gospels through the Wrong Lens

The story of Jesus is found in the gospel records of Matthew, Mark, Luke, and John. The four gospels give us the narrative details of our Lord's birth, life, crucifixion, resurrection, and ascension—events that form the central, pivotal movements of the *historia salutis*, the history of salvation. These are the non-recurring historical events through which God has brought redemption to the world.[2] While redemptive history also includes the epochal events of the Old Testament (e.g., God's covenant with Abraham, the exodus of Israel from Egypt, etc.), the divine plan reaches its climax in Jesus.

One of my goals in this book is to help you read the story of Jesus in the gospel narratives in a gospel-centered way. I already see the raised eyebrow. You may scratch your head and wonder how a book like this could be useful, much less necessary. The need for a gospel-centered approach to the Old Testament may seem more obvious, but can we actually read the Gospels in a non-gospel-centered way? The answer is yes. It is possible to read the Gospels (the books of Matthew, Mark, Luke, and John) and miss *the gospel* (the good news of God's saving work in Jesus).

Consider an illustration. Since adolescence, I've had a degenerative eye disorder called keratoconus. The exact cause of keratoconus is unknown, but the condition involves the thinning of the cornea. The cornea normally has a spherical shape, but in keratoconus the thinning cornea develops a cone-like shape that deflects light entering the eye, resulting in severe nearsightedness, astigmatism, sensitivity to light, and distortions of vision. In my case, the best treatment for keratoconus is wearing gas permeable contact lenses. Without these lenses my vision is severely limited: I cannot drive safely or discern the facial expressions of my children sitting across the table. I can read only by closing one eye and holding the book a few inches from my face. Even a pair of strong glasses is insufficient to help me see with clarity.

Many people approach the Gospels with something like spiritual keratoconus. While they may perceive spiritual light, they don't see clearly because they lack the proper theological lenses. True believers, of course, desire to know and serve Christ, so they reach for spectacles and start reading. But the lenses in their glasses are often too weak to provide sufficient clarity.

Some people, for example, read the Gospels through the lens of *inspiring stories*. They see stirring accounts of people whose lives were changed by Jesus. Guilty people were forgiven. The sick were healed. Blind men regained their sight. A widow's son was raised to life. The hungry multitudes were fed. And these stories *are* inspiring. But if you read the Gospels and conclude, "Maybe if I have enough faith, Jesus will heal me too," you're missing the main point.

Others read the Gospels through the lens of *imitation*. This lens views Jesus as a positive moral role model. Jesus was baptized: you should be baptized. Jesus defeated the devil's temptations with the sword of the Spirit, the word of God: you should therefore memorize lots of Scripture so you can fight temptation the same way. Jesus fed the hungry: go and do likewise. In other words, Jesus is first and foremost an example to follow, a pattern to copy, a model to imitate. And, of course, Jesus *is* our example. John, Peter, and Paul, each in their own ways, teach us to imitate Christ, to follow him, to become like him. But if the example of Jesus is the only thing you see when you read the Gospels, it will not save you. Rather, it will devastate you. The stories of Jesus will become law, not gospel. Bad news, not good news.

Still others read the Gospels through the lens of *information*. This is where the Bible student or scholar comes in. The student's interest is sometimes more detached and academic, but she knows there is something unique about the gospel narratives. Her main goal in reading is not to be inspired, but informed. So she focuses on gleaning interesting historical details and mining important doctrinal nuggets from the text. Of course, just as there is some usefulness to the other approaches as well, there's nothing wrong with this as far as it goes. We must simply recognize that it is easy to amass a wealth of information while remaining spiritual paupers.

Most people do not realize that they read the Gospels in these ways. We just use the glasses nearby without thinking much about them. What I've found as a pastor is that inspiration, imitation, and information are sometimes the only sets of lenses well-meaning people have for reading the stories of Jesus. But these lenses aren't nearly strong enough.

The Gospel Lens: Union with Christ

We need to read the Gospels through what I'm calling "the gospel lens." That lens is the doctrine of our union with Christ, which the twentieth-century Scottish professor John Murray called "the central truth of the whole doctrine of salvation."[3] What is this union? We find it woven through Scripture in five strands:

1. Believers are "in Christ" and "with Christ." The apostle Paul uses the phrase "in Christ" and its equivalents dozens of times in his letters. Many of his letters begin with a greeting to the saints who are located in a given geographical location (Corinth, Ephesus, etc.) and who are also "sanctified in Christ Jesus" (1 Cor. 1:2), "faithful in Christ Jesus" (Eph. 1:1), or simply "in Christ" (Phil. 1:1; Col. 1:2; cf. 1 Thess. 1:1; 2 Thess. 1:1). Paul begins Ephesians with a hymn-like paean of praise to God the Father for blessing us "in Christ with every spiritual blessing in the heavenly places" (Eph. 1:3). These blessings include being chosen in him (v. 4), blessed (literally, graced) in him (v. 6), redeemed and forgiven in him (v. 7), united in him (v. 10), given an inheritance in him (v. 11), predestined in him (v. 11), and sealed by the Spirit in him (v. 13). The various phrases "in Christ," "in Christ Jesus," and "in him" occur more than twenty times in Ephesians alone.

   The similar phrases "with Christ" and "with him" also appear frequently in Paul's letters. Paul describes believers as those who

- have been crucified with Christ (Gal. 2:20),
- have died with Christ (Rom. 6:8; Col. 2:20),
- are buried with Christ (Rom. 6:4; Col. 2:12),
- are made alive with Christ (Eph. 2:5; Col. 2:13),
- are raised with Christ (Eph. 2:6; Col. 2:12; 3:1; cf. also Rom. 6:4),
- are seated with Christ (Eph. 2:6),
- are hidden with Christ (Col. 3:3),
- are fellow heirs with Christ (Rom. 8:17),
- and will appear with Christ in glory (Col. 3:4).

2. Christ is with us because he became a human like us.
Passages about the incarnation include the nativity stories in Matthew and Luke, the magnificent prologue to John's gospel, and the apostolic reflection on Christ's incarnation in the New Testament letters. Over and again, the Scriptures declare the mystery of how God the Son took our nature:

- "And the Word became flesh and dwelt among us, and we have seen his glory, glory as of the only Son from the Father, full of grace and truth" (John 1:14).
- "For God has done what the law, weakened by the flesh, could not do. By sending his own Son in the likeness of sinful flesh and for sin, he condemned sin in the flesh, in order that the righteous requirement of the law might be fulfilled in us, who walk not according to the flesh but according to the Spirit" (Rom. 8:3–4).
- "Since therefore the children share in flesh and blood, he himself likewise partook of the same things, that through death he might destroy the one who has the power of death, that is, the devil, and deliver all those who through fear of death were subject to lifelong slavery" (Heb. 2:14–15).

As we will see in chapter one, the doctrine of Christ's incarnation is foundational to our salvation. We can only be united to Christ in his saving benefits if he is united to us in our human nature.

3. The Bible gives us rich and helpful pictures of our union with Christ. For example, in Ephesians 5, we find the *marital* metaphor. Paul exhorts husbands to love their wives "as Christ loved the church and gave himself up for her" (Eph. 5:25), for marriage is a "mystery" that "refers to Christ and the church" (v. 32). Paul also uses a *biological* metaphor, describing us as members of a body, with Christ as our head. In Ephesians 1:22–23, Paul tells us that God has "put all things under [Christ's] feet and gave him as head over all things to the church, which is his body, the fullness of him who fills all in all" (cf. Eph. 4:15–16, 5:23, 30; Col. 1:18, 24; 2:19).

The apostle Peter uses the *architectural* metaphor of a temple, where the church is built on Christ as the cornerstone while the members themselves are "living stones" that comprise the temple (see 1 Peter 2:4–8; cf. 1 Cor. 3:16–17; Eph. 2:19–22). And in a passage we will revisit in chapter 6, Jesus employed the *agricultural* metaphor of branches that bear fruit only by abiding in Christ, the true vine (John 15:1–6). Each picture teaches something unique and specific, but all of them illustrate the truth that believers are somehow united to Christ.

4. Christ is with us through covenant. The covenantal language found in both the Old Testament and the New reveals how Christ is our representative.[4] The Lord Jesus, as the great shepherd, shed his blood according to an eternal covenant (Heb. 13:20), a pact or agreement made between the Father and the Son before the foundation of the world. In this covenant, the Father gave the Son a people to

redeem (John 6:37; 17:6–9) and entrusted to him the work of salvation (John 17:5).

The Son's role in this work is analogous to that of Adam, the first father and representative of humanity. As Adam's disobedience led to sin and death for all, so the obedience of Christ leads to righteousness and life for all who receive God's gift (Rom. 5:12–21; cf. 1 Cor. 15:21–22, 45–49). We might think of Adam and Christ as the "team captains" of the human race. Adam the First fumbled the fall and lost the game for us all, while Adam the Second singlehandedly carried the ball to the finish line, winning life for all who are in him. As Paul says in Romans 5:17, "For if, because of one man's trespass, death reigned through that one man, much more will those who receive the abundance of grace and the free gift of righteousness reign in life through the one man Jesus Christ." In Sinclair Ferguson's succinct summary, "Christ appeared as 'Adam in reverse,' undoing what Adam did, regaining what Adam lost, restoring to man what was forfeited by Adam."[5]

The theme of covenant is also prominent in the book of Hebrews, which describes the supremacy of God's Son to all the figures and forms of the old covenant—that is, the covenant God made with Israel in the Old Testament. For example, Jesus is shown to be supreme over prophets (Heb. 1:1–2), angels (1:4–2:18), Moses (3:1–6), and Joshua (3:7–4:11). Moreover, he is our great high priest, superior to the entire order of the priesthood in the old covenant (4:12–7:28) because he has a better ministry and has made a better sacrifice enacted on better promises based on a better covenant (Heb. 8–10). This covenant is the "new covenant" of which Jeremiah wrote (Jer. 31:31; Heb. 8:8–13) and which Jesus himself inaugurated in his blood-shedding death (Luke 22:20). At the heart of this covenant is this double agreement: the Son agrees *with the Father* that he will unite to himself our human nature so as to fully obey the law in our place and bear our sins on his shoulders; and he agrees *with us* to be our substitute and representative.

5. Finally, we are actually united to Christ in personal experience. The New Testament offers various ways to understand how this happens. For example, Scripture over and over again says that we believe "into" (*eis*) Christ (John 3:16; Rom. 10:14; Gal. 2:16; Phil. 1:29). These passages teach us that we are united to Christ through faith. Other passages speak of our receiving Christ (John 1:12; Col. 2:6) and his dwelling in us (John 14:20; Col. 3:17), and still others of being baptized into Christ (Rom. 6:3; Gal. 3:27). These latter passages do not mean that the act of baptism itself joins us to Christ apart from faith, but rather (as the larger context of Rom. 6:1–14 indicates) that baptism is the sign, symbol, and seal of our faith-union with Christ in his death and resurrection.[6] Lying behind our faith is the prior work of the Holy Spirit, whose creative energies bring us from death to life through the miracle of regeneration or new birth (John 3:3–8; Titus 3:5). "Our union with the Lord," writes Ferguson, "is created by the agency of the Holy Spirit."[7] And the result of this union is nothing less than a new creation, which is why Paul can say, "Therefore, if anyone is in Christ, he is a new creation. The old has passed away; behold, the new has come" (2 Cor. 5:17).

As you can see from this brief survey, this glorious theme of union with Christ is pervasive in the New Testament, particularly in the writings of the apostle Paul. Sinclair Ferguson suggests that Paul's outworking of this theme was a direct result of Christ's initial revelation of himself on the Damascus road.[8] Do you remember what Jesus said to Paul there? "Saul, Saul, why are you persecuting *me*?" (Acts 9:4). Saul was persecuting the church, but the risen Lord's words to Saul revealed the profound union that binds Christ to his people. As the Reformer John Calvin wrote:

Christ is not outside us but dwells within us. Not only does he cleave to us by an indivisible bond of fellowship, but with a wonderful communion, day by day, he grows more and more into one body with us, until he becomes completely one with us.[9]

We therefore can and should read the gospel narratives through this lens of our union with Christ. This is not merely an academic exercise in theology. As a pastor, I want to help people change and grow. In Paul's words, my aim is to see Christ formed in you (Gal. 4:19).[10] God's purpose in salvation is to conform us to the image of his Son (Rom. 8:29). But he has appointed means for achieving this design— namely, the work of his Spirit through the ministry of the gospel as we behold the glory of Christ (2 Cor. 3:18). Beholding Christ's glory is what this book is about. Transformation into his glorious image is the desired outcome. And reading the life of Christ through the lens of union with Christ is the means to that end.[11]

Christ for Us, We with Christ

This book evolved from a series of sermons first preached in 2014. I developed those messages while reading a nineteenth-century Scottish theologian named Hugh Martin, whom the Lord used along with Dr. Sinclair Ferguson (also a Scot!) to help me unearth a rich vein of theological gold in studying the life of Christ. In particular, these men helped me read the gospel narratives through the theological lens of union with Christ.

It was not that I had never thought about this doctrine. In fact, one of my earlier books includes significant discussion of this important theme.[12] But further study, guided in part by Martin and Ferguson, has sharpened my focus on Christ's accomplishments for his people—not only in his death and resurrection, but also in his birth and life. And more than ever before, I have become gripped with this glorious truth: that in all of his obedience, Jesus was acting as our representative, husband, and head. If I am in Christ, then his achievements are counted as mine. What he accomplished, I accomplished with him.

So I want to invite you on a journey through the climatic events in the life of Jesus. We will trace Jesus' steps through the most important stories.

With shepherds and angels, we will worship the infant Jesus wrapped in swaddling clothes in a Bethlehem manger. We will hear the Father's heavenly affirmation of his Son following his baptism in the Jordan River. We will observe Christ our Captain as he battles the evil one in the Judean desert. We will gaze on Christ's glorious face as he is transfigured in the glory cloud on Mt. Hermon. We will hear the shouts of "Hosanna!" as pilgrims accompany the humble Messiah into the city of Jerusalem. We will learn from the Master as he teaches his disciples in the upper room. We will watch as the Man of Sorrows wrestles with grief in the Gethsemane garden. We will witness the travesty of justice as Jesus is falsely charged in the courts of men. We will consider the crucified Christ as he drinks the cup of wrath and bears the dreadful curse on Calvary's tree. We will gladden our hearts as we ponder the meaning of Christ's empty tomb. We will lift up eyes of faith as Jesus ascends to the right hand of God. And we will fuel our hope with the promise of his glorious return.[13]

These are familiar events in the life of Jesus. But as we study them, I want to probe their relevance for us today, as believers joined to him through faith. I want you to understand that what Jesus did in these critical moments, he did for us—for you and for me. I want you to know that if you are united to Jesus through faith and by the Spirit, then in a very real sense you were *with Jesus* ...

- in the manger
- in the river
- in the desert
- on the mountain
- in the city
- in the upper room
- in the garden
- in the court
- and on the tree

So now you are raised with the risen Christ in his resurrection life. Now, you are seated with the ascended Christ in the heavens. And when he appears, you will also appear with him in glory.

1

With Jesus in the Manger: *Birth*

"Behold, the virgin shall conceive and bear a son, and they shall
call his name Immanuel" (which means, God with us).

Matthew 1:23

Every December, hundreds of people flood concert halls and
performing arts centers to attend live productions of Handel's
Messiah, one of the most loved and enduring works of classical music.
The Lutheran composer George Frideric Handel wrote the stirring
music in just twenty-four days, from August 22 to September 14,
1741, and then suffered criticism from religious people before they
even heard the first note. The fact that the first performance of the
oratorio would occur in a Dublin theater rather than a church seemed
downright scandalous. One wonders what those same critics would
think today, when many churches rent theaters for weekly worship!
But despite early concern, Handel's *Messiah* lives on. In fact, it has
been performed at least once somewhere around the globe every
year since its 1742 debut.[1]

The most remarkable thing about the *Messiah,* however, is not
its fast composition or its enduring popularity, but the beauty of its
music and its subject matter. The memorable melodies tell the great
story of salvation through Jesus Christ, this drama that is the heart

of the gospel and the cornerstone of our faith. Arranged in three "acts," the *Messiah* libretto is comprised of fifty-three passages of Scripture, which move from the prophetic hopes for the Messiah in the Old Testament to his birth in Bethlehem, through his passion, resurrection, and ascension, to the resurrection of the saints at his second coming and the dawn of his eternal reign. *Messiah* embraces the most significant movements of redemptive history in sometimes breathtaking coloratura and choral majesty.

The core of Handel's *Messiah* is the doctrine of the incarnation,[2] which the Dutch theologian Herman Bavinck later called "the central fact of the entire history of the world."[3] Indeed, the only way Jesus could deliver us from the power of death and welcome us into his family was to take on flesh and blood himself. Through the incarnation, the Son assumed human nature, sanctified it, and won redemption for us *as one of us* (see Heb. 2:7–18). His union with us in our humanity makes possible our union with him in grace.[4]

How did the Son become human? He was conceived by the power of the Holy Spirit and born of the virgin Mary. But even before his birth, Jesus was destined for a unique life and death. He was born in humility, born under the law, born to save the world.

Jesus Was Born in Humility

The record of our Lord's nativity is striking in its simplicity. But, then, the earthly circumstances of his birth were truly modest, humble, and ordinary. Jesus was born into a family from Nazareth of Galilee (Luke 2:4a). Not Rome, the grand and stately capital of the Empire, impressive in military might. Not Athens, the center of art and learning in the ancient world. Not even Jerusalem, the religious center of Israel. But podunk little Nazareth. This posed a stumbling block for at least one disciple (John 1:45–46), though it fulfilled prophecy (Isaiah 9:1).

At birth, Jesus' mother "wrapped him in swaddling cloths and laid him in a manger, because there was no place for them in the inn" (Luke 2:7). The word "inn" might be better understood as a guest room rather than a motel, though in the ancient world, such a space would regularly house animals at night, which explains why this one had a manger, or a feeding trough.[5]

Not an ideal crib, but a functional one. The "swaddling cloths," which served as a sign to the shepherds, the first witnesses and worshipers of the infant Savior King (Luke 2:12), also indicated the humble conditions of Jesus' birth.

These external features underscore the divine humility in the incarnation itself. The divine and eternal Word who created all things (John 1:1–3) became flesh: a tiny embryo nurtured in a woman's womb to be born in the way any child is born, pushing and screaming his way into life. And upon birth, Jesus continued the ordinary process of development and growth. He was fully dependent on his mother's milk for life and nourishment. He relied on his parents' tender care

The Chalcedonian Creed (AD 451)

The average Christian loves Jesus but doesn't spend much time thinking about Christology. Why does that matter? We may affirm that Jesus is both fully God and fully man, but we often forget (or have never been told) that the church spent the better part of five centuries hammering out just what that means.

In AD 451, the Fourth Ecumenical Council in Asia Minor adopted the definitive creedal statement on the two natures of Christ. The Chalcedonian Creed countered a number of christological heresies plaguing the first half-century of the church and embraced the "two nature, one person" formula, which became the standard way of expressing the "hypostatic union" of Christ's divine and human natures in one person.

"Following the holy fathers, we all with one accord teach men to acknowledge one and the same Son, our Lord Jesus Christ, at once complete in divinity and complete in manhood, truly God and truly man, consisting also of a rational soul and body; of one substance [*homoousios*] with the Father as regards his Godhead, and at the same time of one substance with us as regards his manhood; like us in all respects, apart from sin; as regards his Godhead, begotten of the Father before the ages, but yet as regards his manhood begotten [born], for us men and for our salvation, of Mary the virgin, the God-bearer [*theotokos*]; one and the same Christ, Son, Lord, only-begotten, recognized in two natures, without confusion, without change, without division, without separation; the distinction of natures being in no way annulled by the union, but rather the characteristics of each nature being preserved and coming together to form one person and subsistence [*hypostasis*], not as parted or separated into two persons, but one and the same Son and only-begotten God the Word, Lord Jesus Christ."[6]

for protection from the elements and on their guidance as he grew into childhood and adulthood.[7]

Astounding! God manifested in the flesh. *God, the baby.* God whose diapers must be changed, who must be burped after feeding, who must be potty trained. I don't write this to be irreverent, but to draw attention to the astonishing scandal, the perplexing mystery, the gracious beauty of the incarnation. Nor do I mean that the divine *nature* itself was subject to this humiliation. We recognize two natures, human and divine, united in the one person of Christ. He is the eternal Word who united himself to human nature in the incarnation. Yet, the Son of God is not two persons, but one. This Person was born among us. Therefore, just as Paul can speak of the church being purchased by God's blood (Acts 20:28), so we can, in truth, describe the incarnation as God's birth.

Jesus Was Born under the Law

Not only was Jesus born in humility, Jesus was also born under the law. This is implied throughout his birth accounts, for Jesus was born into a Jewish family. But it is explicit in Luke 2:21–24, where we learn that Jesus was circumcised on the eighth day, named "Jesus" in accord with the prior angelic announcement, and then brought to Jerusalem and presented to God in accord with the Law. Luke gives considerable detail to these events, referencing the law three times ("the Law of Moses" in v. 22, "the Law of the Lord" in vv. 23 and 24). Perhaps Luke was thinking Paul's words: "But when the fullness of time had come, God sent forth his Son, born of woman, born under the law, to redeem those who were under the law, so that we might receive adoption as sons" (Gal. 4:4–5).

Why was Jesus' birth under the law so important? In those verses from Galatians, Paul writes that in order to redeem those under the law, the Son had to be born under the law himself.[8] Only by fulfilling the law perfectly in our place could Jesus rescue us from our law breaking and adopt us into God's family.

In his magnificent meditation on the glory of Christ, Puritan pastor and theologian John Owen wrote of how Jesus acted as our mediator. The obedience of Christ, according to Owen, "was not for himself, but *for us*.[9] We were obligated to keep the law but could not. The eternal Son of God was not obligated to keep the law, but in his incarnation, he freely chose to be born under (and keep) the law, in our place, so that "by the one man's obedience the many will be made righteous" (Rom. 5:19b).

Jesus Was Born to Save the World

Finally, Jesus was born to save the world. Luke indicates this in the opening chapters of his narrative in several ways. Gabriel's angelic visit to Mary in Luke 1:26–38 teaches us of Jesus' virginal conception by the Holy Spirit (vv. 27, 34–35), the sanctification of his human nature (v. 35), his messianic identity as the son of David and heir to the Davidic throne (vv. 32–33), Mary's initial perplexity upon receiving this news (vv. 29–30), and her humble submission to God's will (v. 38). We also learn how Gabriel instructed Mary to name her son "Jesus"—a name pointing to his role as Savior (Matt. 1:21).

Question 35: What does it mean that he "was conceived by the Holy Spirit and born of the virgin Mary"?

Answer: That the eternal Son of God, who is and remains true and eternal God, took to himself, through the working of the Holy Spirit, from the flesh and blood of the virgin Mary, a truly human nature so that he might also become David's true descendant, like his brothers and sisters in every way except for sin.

Question 36: How does the holy conception and birth of Christ benefit you?

Answer: He is our mediator and, in God's sight, he covers with his innocence and perfect holiness my sinfulness in which I was conceived.

—The Heidelberg Catechism

I think the most interesting insight in this account concerns the Holy Spirit's role in Jesus' conception and birth. Luke 1:35 not only teaches the miraculous nature of Jesus' conception,[10] but also highlights the special work of the Holy Spirit in the incarnation. The word "overshadow" is a clue to the underlying theological mystery. As Darrell L. Bock observes, overshadowing in the Old Testament "refers either to the Shekinah cloud that rested on the tabernacle (Ex. 40:34–35; Num. 9:18; 10:34) or to God's presence in protecting his people (Ps. 91:4; 140:7)."[11] The word also alludes to the creation narrative, when "the Spirit of God was *hovering* over the face of the waters" (Gen. 1:2). Just as God's Spirit brooded over the primordial waters on the eve of creation, so now he overshadows the darkness of Mary's womb on the eve of new creation.

Pax Romana or *Pax Christiana*?

The peace proclaimed by the angelic host and secured through the incarnate Christ stands in stark contrast to the peace offered by the world. Luke's first readers were well acquainted with that kind of peace because they inhabited a world dominated by the Roman Empire and therefore its promise of *Pax Romana*.

Note that Luke addressed his Gospel to the "most excellent Theophilus" (1:3), who may have been a Roman dignitary. He then begins the narrative of Jesus' birth with the decree of Caesar Augustus (Luke 2:1), the adopted son of Julius Caesar. Following a violent civil war, Augustus had become the first emperor of the Roman Empire, reigning from 27 BC until his death in AD 14. Augustus's birth was hailed as the birthday of a god, which marked the beginning of the good news (*euangellion*).[13] And after his ascension to the throne, Augustus declared that he had brought peace and justice to the world. For the next 250 years, the rule of Rome would be called the *Pax Romana*, or *peace of Rome*.

While some would celebrate this propaganda, others saw through the façade. The Roman historian Tacitus, for example, understood that for conquered nations the *Pax Romana* was a threat better regarded as *Vis Romana*, or *power of Rome*.[14] The peace of Rome, after all, was secured and enforced through violence. It came on the sharp point of bloody Roman swords.

The *shalom* foretold by prophets and heralded by angels came differently—not from a Roman Caesar, but from the humble and incarnate Son of God. This peace—the *Pax Christiana*, or *peace of Christ*—wasn't secured at the expense of justice through the violent conquest and overthrow of nations, but through the self-substitution of Christ, in whose death righteousness and peace kissed each other (Ps. 85:10). God's peace came not by the edge of the sword, but through Christ's loving self-sacrifice on a bloody cross. "For in him all the fullness of God was pleased to dwell, and through him to reconcile to himself all things, whether on earth or in heaven, making peace by the blood of his cross" (Col. 1:19–20).

Luke will use this language again in the story of Jesus' transfiguration (Luke 9:34). And he will again echo creation in chapter 3, first when the Spirit descends on the baptized Jesus "in bodily form, like a dove" (Luke 3:22) and again when Luke traces the baby Jesus' genealogy not just to Abraham, but to "Adam, the son of God" (Luke 3:38). Deftly woven into the fabric of Luke's gospel, these details underline the centrality of the incarnation to God's redemptive plan for the renewal and restoration of creation. As Letham writes, "The incarnation should not be seen as merely a *means* to salvation. Rather, salvation finds its ultimate fulfillment in the union of humanity with God seen in the incarnate Christ."[12]

The angels also highlight Jesus' role as Savior when they announce his birth to the shepherds:

> And an angel of the Lord appeared to them, and the glory of the Lord shone around them, and they were filled with great fear. And the angel said to them, "Fear not, for behold, I bring you good news of great joy that will be for all the people. For unto you is born this day in the city of David a Savior, who is Christ the Lord.... And suddenly there was with the angel a multitude of the heavenly host praising God and saying, "Glory to God in the highest, and on earth peace among those with whom he is pleased."
>
> Luke 2:9–11, 13–14

Verse 14 spells out both the purpose and nature of this salvation: the *purpose* of salvation is "glory to God in the highest" and the *nature* of this salvation is "peace on earth" (KJV). Thus, God connects his glorious purpose with the good of mankind. As Jonathan Edwards persuasively reasoned over 300 years ago, God's own glory is his ultimate end in all of his works, including salvation.[15] Here, we see that he accomplishes his own glory by establishing *shalom*, which is "the webbing together of God, humans, and all creation in justice, fulfillment, and delight."[16] Peace is more than just a tranquil feeling or a cease-fire; peace is the full restoration of cosmic harmony in every domain of creaturely existence. Peace is fullness of life under the healing, redeeming reign of God. It is life in the kingdom of God. And Luke 2 tells us that Jesus came to accomplish exactly that.

We began this chapter remembering that Handel's *Messiah* is not simply stunning music with enduring popularity but that its libretto centers on the mystery of the incarnation. This mystery is revealed in the humble circumstances of our Lord's birth, the union of his divine and human natures, and the saving purpose of his incarnation. But the culmination of this mystery carries us from the manger all the way to the cross. The Christ child was born to die so that we could live.

2

With Jesus in the River: *Baptism*

> Then Jesus came from Galilee to the Jordan to John, to be
> baptized by him. John would have prevented him, saying, "I
> need to be baptized by you, and do you come to me?" But Jesus
> answered him, "Let it be so now, for thus it is fitting for us to
> fulfill all righteousness." Then he consented.
>
> Matthew 3:13–15

Have you ever wondered why Jesus insisted on being baptized?
Raised in a Baptist home, I always assumed he was baptized as our
example. Since Jesus was baptized, we certainly should be baptized
(by immersion, no less!) as well.

But nowhere do the Scriptures exhort us to be baptized on
the basis of Christ's example. Not once. Not by the disciples. Not
in the sermons of Peter in the book of Acts. Not in the letters of
Paul. Not by Jesus himself. This doesn't mean that Jesus' baptism has
no exemplary value. But that's not the focus Scripture gives to the
baptism of our Lord.

To grasp the significance of Jesus' baptism, we must grapple with
the story narrated in the Gospels. Matthew tells us that Jesus came to
be baptized by John the Baptist and that John's baptism was a baptism
of repentance: "Then Jerusalem and all Judea and all the region about

the Jordan were going out to him, and they were baptized by him in the river Jordan, confessing their sins" (3:5–6). Then he says that when Jesus came for baptism, John protested (v. 14). Matthew uses the iterative, imperfect verb to stress John's repeated attempts to keep Jesus from being baptized.[1] Again and again, John says, "No, Jesus. Don't ask me to do this!"

Why was John reluctant? Because baptism was a rite of repentance. It implied cleansing from sin, turning from one's old ways, starting new. Prior to John's ministry, Gentiles were baptized when they converted as proselytes of Judaism, but Jews rarely submitted to the symbolic cleansing. Then John came on the stage exhorting the Jews—God's own people—to repent and be baptized. People heeded John's call by the hundreds.

Enter Jesus. "John, baptize me." Of course, John protested. Somehow he knew that Jesus, of all people, didn't need his baptism. Jesus didn't need to repent. He had no sins to turn from, no evil from which to be cleansed.

"Don't make me do this, Jesus," he said. "This isn't right. You shouldn't be here. I need to be baptized by you, not you by me." Jesus responded, "Let it be so now, for thus it is fitting for us to fulfill all righteousness" (v. 15). What did Jesus mean? What was going on? Jesus' words and the events that followed revealed why his baptism was necessary and important. It accomplished four things: fulfillment, identification, representation, and anointing.

Fulfillment

"Let it be so now, for thus it is fitting for us to *fulfill* all righteousness." The word *fulfill* is significant in Matthew, and *fulfillment* is an important theme in his narrative. Matthew frequently notes how something "took place to fulfill what was spoken by the prophet" (cf. 1:22; 2:15, 17, 23; 4:14; 8:17; 12:17; 13:14, 35; 21:4; 26:56; 27:9).[2] But Jesus not only fulfilled specific Messianic prophecies; he also embodied and fulfilled the typological patterns of Old Testament history. For example, in Matthew 2, Joseph, Mary, and the baby Jesus fled from Judea to Egypt to escape the murderous plots of King Herod. Matthew then quotes the prophet Hosea, who wrote that

God called his son from Egypt. Hosea was recalling the events of the exodus.

What happened to Israel following their release from Egypt? They passed through the Red Sea and spent forty years in the wilderness. In the same way, Jesus passes through the waters (Matt. 3) to be tempted for forty days in the desert (Matt. 4:1–17). Thus, Matthew quotes Hosea to show how Jesus embodied Israel. Jesus was living Israel's story and bringing it to fulfillment. Jesus was called out of Egypt *as the new Israel who will lead God's people on a new exodus.*

Identification

Baptism is and always has been a rite of identification. When the masses were baptized in the Jordan, they were identifying themselves as sinners in need of God's cleansing and forgiveness. When new believers are baptized in the name of the Father, Son, and Holy Spirit (Matt. 28:19), they are identifying themselves as disciples of Jesus. When Paul speaks of baptism, he connects it to putting on Christ (Gal. 3:27) and being united to Christ in his death, burial, and resurrection (Rom. 6:3–4). Indeed, in the early centuries of the church, when people were baptized, they received a new set of clothes and a new name, symbolizing their new identity in Christ.

Jesus' baptism was also a rite of identification. He was identifying himself with the people he came to redeem. "He undertook to share baptism with us," writes Calvin, "that the faithful might be more surely persuaded that they are ingrafted into His body, buried with Him in baptism, that they may rise again to newness of life."[3]

But we cannot ignore that John's baptism was a baptism of repentance, a rite of washing and cleansing for sinners. Everyone knew that, and Jesus received exactly that.[4] Though Jesus himself wasn't guilty of any sins, he came to be the friend and Savior of sinners. Jesus' immersion in the muddy waters of the Jordan previewed his immersion into the fiery deluge of God's wrath against sin. "I came to cast fire on the earth, and would that it were already kindled!" Jesus would later say. "I have a baptism to be baptized with, and how great is my distress until it is accomplished!" (Luke 12:50). So at the inauguration of his ministry, Jesus identifies himself with the very sinners he came to redeem. Sinners are not here taking the name of Jesus. Rather, Jesus takes the name of sinners. He identifies himself with them.

Yet another identification takes place following his baptism:

> And when Jesus was baptized, immediately he went up from the water, and behold, the heavens were opened to him, and he saw the Spirit of God descending like a dove and coming to rest on him; and behold, a voice from heaven said, "This is my beloved Son, with whom I am well pleased."
>
> Matthew 3:16–17

We dare not miss the significance of the divine voice speaking from the opened heavens. Jewish rabbis of the first century believed that God's voice had not been heard since the days of the prophets Haggai, Zechariah, and Malachi. God had been silent for 400 years! But now, as Jesus emerges from the water, the heavens are torn open (Mark 1:10, with an allusion to Isa. 64:1) and the Father speaks. What does he say? "This is my beloved Son, with whom I am well pleased." He identifies Jesus as his own Son. The Father's words echo Messianic prophecy by alluding to two Old Testament verses: Psalm 2:7, which looked forward to God's Son as the Messianic king, and Isaiah 42:1, which expressed God's delight in the enigmatic servant of the Lord. So the Father, in an extraordinary speech following an extraordinary baptism, identifies his Son as both royal king and suffering servant— exactly what his people needed.[5]

Representation

When Jesus was baptized in the Jordan River he was not simply fulfilling the prophetic types of the Old Testament. Neither was he merely identifying himself with the sinners he came to save. He was also representing them. He was fulfilling all righteousness on the behalf of his covenant people.

This is evident in how this passage and the rest of Matthew's gospel use the prophet Isaiah's words about the servant of the Lord. We have already seen how Matthew 3:16–17 describes the heavens opening, the Spirit descending, and the Father pronouncing his delight in the Son with words that recall Isaiah 42:1. Jesus has already said that he must be baptized in order to "fulfill all righteousness," perhaps alluding to Isaiah 53:11 where the Lord's servant is called the "righteous one" who will "make many to be accounted righteous" by bearing their iniquities. Matthew continues to develop this theme throughout his gospel, skillfully weaving threads from Isaiah into the tapestry of his narrative concerning Jesus.

In chapter 8, after Jesus heals many of illnesses and demons, Matthew says this fulfills Isaiah 53:4. In chapter 12, Matthew connects Jesus' compassionate healing of a man's withered arm with the servant who refuses to break the bruised reed or quench the smoldering wick (Matt. 12:17–21; c.f., Isa. 42:1–4). But Matthew seems to have Isaiah 53 primarily in mind as he writes. Prior to Jesus' entry into Jerusalem and the beginning of his passion, Jesus teaches his disciples about servanthood by describing himself as the Son of Man who ransoms his people (see Matt. 20:28). Finally, on the night of his betrayal, as Jesus eats the last Passover meal with his disciples, he again echoes the language of Isaiah 53 about the servant who "poured out his soul to death and was numbered with the transgressors," and who "bore the sin of many, and makes intercession for the transgressors" (v. 12).

Jesus viewed himself as the servant of the Lord who would come to represent God's people, bear their sins, and give his life as a ransom on their behalf. But how would he fulfill this calling? And what would he accomplish for his people as a result? We have seen his fulfillment, identification, and representation, but to answer these questions, we consider his anointing.

Anointing

Matthew 3:16 is one of the clearest passages on the Trinity in all of Scripture, for we see all three members of the Trinity active at the same time in different ways to accomplish the same event: "And when Jesus was baptized, immediately he went up from the water, and behold, the heavens were opened to him, and he saw the Spirit of God descending like a dove and coming to rest on him." Here, the Son is baptized, the Spirit descends, and the Father speaks. As Jerome, one of the church fathers, wrote, "The mystery of the Trinity is revealed in the baptism."[6] This is a pattern that will occur again and again in the life and ministry of Jesus, as he does the will of the Father in the power of the Spirit.

Notice how the Spirit descended upon Jesus "like a dove." In Luke 3:22 we read that the Spirit descended on him "in bodily form, like a dove." When we read this, we should remember how the Spirit hovered over the waters in the creation narrative of Genesis 1:2. But here, he appears as a dove to signify the inauguration of new creation in the ministry of Jesus. As we will see in the next chapter, Jesus came not only as the Messiah of Israel, but also as the second Adam, the head of new creation.

> **Question 31:** Why is he called "Christ," meaning "anointed"?
>
> **Answer:** Because he has been ordained by God the Father and has been anointed with the Holy Spirit to be our chief prophet and teacher who fully reveals to us the secret counsel and will of God concerning our deliverance; our only high priest who has delivered us by the one sacrifice of his body, and who continually pleads our cause with the Father; and our eternal king who governs us by his Word and Spirit, and who guards us and keeps us in the freedom he has won for us.
>
> —*The Heidelberg Catechism*

The Spirit not only descends on Jesus, he *rests upon him*. Once again, the prophet Isaiah helps us understand what is happening. Consider three passages:

> There shall come forth a shoot from the stump of Jesse,
> and a branch from his roots shall bear fruit.
> And the Spirit of the Lord shall rest upon him,
>
> the Spirit of wisdom and understanding,
> the Spirit of counsel and might,
> the Spirit of knowledge and the fear of the Lord.
>
> Isaiah 11:1–2

Behold my servant, whom I uphold,
my chosen, in whom my soul delights;
I have put my Spirit upon him;
he will bring forth justice to the nations.

Isaiah 42:1

The Spirit of the Lord God is upon me,
because the Lord has anointed me
to bring good news to the poor;
he has sent me to bind up the brokenhearted,
to proclaim liberty to the captives,
and the opening of the prison to those who are bound;
to proclaim the year of the Lord's favor,
and the day of vengeance of our God;
to comfort all who mourn;
to grant to those who mourn in Zion—
to give them a beautiful headdress instead of ashes,
the oil of gladness instead of mourning,
the garment of praise instead of a faint spirit;
that they may be called oaks of righteousness,
the planting of the Lord, that he may be glorified.

Isaiah 61:1–3

In each passage, Isaiah looks forward to someone who will be uniquely anointed and equipped with the Spirit of the Lord. Jesus is that person. He is the "shoot from the stump of Jesse," the descendant of David, as Matthew's genealogy of Jesus reveals (Isa. 11:1; Matt. 1:6). He was conceived by the Spirit in the virgin's womb (Isa. 7:14; Matt. 1:18–23). He was the one of whom John spoke in the wilderness, "prepare the way of the Lord" (Isa. 40:3; Matt. 3:3). And now, following Jesus' baptism by John in the Jordan, the Spirit of God descends like a dove and rests upon him (Isa. 42:1; Matt. 3:16). This, then, is how Jesus will fulfill all righteousness as the representative for God's people. He will do so in the power of God's Spirit.

The Spirit's Work in Christ's Human Nature

John Owen, the "Prince of the Puritans" wrote nine books on the Holy Spirit. Yes, nine! Together, these volumes make up a hefty project called *Pneumatologia: A Discourse Concerning the Holy Spirit: Wherein An Account is Given of His Name, Nature, Personality, Dispensation, Operations, and Effects*. (And that's not even the complete title!)

Notwithstanding its density, Owen's work remains the most important book on the Holy Spirit ever written. Some of his richest material concerns the Spirit's work in and on the human nature of Christ. Owen ransacks both Old Testament and New to show that the Spirit worked in no less than ten ways in the life and ministry of Jesus. Here they are in summary:

1. The framing, forming, and miraculous conception of the body of Christ in Mary's womb.
2. The sanctification of Christ's human nature from the moment of its conception.
3. The exercise of grace in Christ's entire life and ministry.
4. The anointing of Christ with all the extraordinary powers and gifts necessary to his offices as prophet, priest, and king.
5. The working of miracles.
6. Guiding, directing, comforting, and supporting Christ in the whole course of his ministry, temptations, obedience, and sufferings.
7. Christ's offering himself as a sacrifice to God on the cross.
8. The preservation of Christ's human nature while his body was in the tomb.
9. Christ's bodily resurrection from the dead.
10. The glorification of Christ's human nature, thus fitting it to reside at God's right hand and making it a pattern for the glorification of all who believe.[7]

It is important that we not miss (or misunderstand) this. Sometimes when we think about Jesus living a life of perfect obedience to God, we think, "Well, of course. But he was God." Yes, Jesus was God. But he didn't obey the Father in the strength of his divine nature, while somehow bypassing his human nature. Jesus didn't cheat on the test by using some hidden divine, superhero-like powers to get through the hard stuff. No, *he obeyed in his humanity*.[8] He felt the same kinds of emotions that you and I feel. Though Jesus never sinned, he faced the same sorts of temptations that we face. His nerves transmitted the same sensations of physical pain to his brain. His human nature was both real and complete. Our salvation hangs on this, for only through sharing our humanity could Jesus break the power of death (Heb. 2:14–15). As the fourth-century church father Gregory of Nazianzus wrote, "that which He has not assumed He has not healed; but that which is united to His Godhead is also saved."[9] Jesus was 100 percent human. He obeyed God, thwarted temptation, fulfilled the law, faced grief, defeated death, and rose from the grave *in our nature*.

So how did he do it? By the Spirit. It is in the fullness of the Spirit's power, and as Israel's anointed king and captain, that Jesus launched into enemy territory to face the onslaughts of the devil (Matt. 4:1–11) and bring justice to the nations (Isa. 42:1–2; Matt. 12:18). It is by the Spirit of God that he ministered to others (Acts 10:38). It is by the Spirit of God that he cast out demons, thus liberating those held captive by Satan (Matt. 12:22–29). When Jesus came to the cross to offer himself as a sacrifice to God, he did so through the Spirit (Heb. 9:14). Then, on the third day, Jesus was "declared to be the Son of God in power according to the Spirit of holiness by his resurrection from the dead" (Rom. 1:4). And when Jesus finally ascended to heaven to take his exalted place at God's right hand, what did he do? He poured out the Spirit on the church (Acts 2:33).

Why do I stress this? Because the same Spirit who anointed, empowered, and equipped Jesus to live in obedience to God has been given to us. The same Spirit who sustained Jesus through his temptations, suffering, and death has been given to us. Jesus has fully obeyed God and fulfilled all righteousness not only in our place, *but also in our nature* by the power of the Spirit. And now he gives the Spirit to us that we may be remade in his own image by the power of the Spirit (2 Cor. 3:18). "From womb to tomb to throne, the Spirit was the constant companion of the Son. As a result, when he comes to Christians to indwell them, he comes as the Spirit of Christ in such a way that to possess him is to possess Christ himself."[10] We are his, and he is ours.

Baptized into Christ Jesus

If you are a believer in Jesus, I hope you have been baptized. If you haven't been baptized, I hope you will be. But as we have seen in this chapter, the baptism of Jesus is far more than a model for you to follow. In fact, when Jesus was baptized by John in the Jordan River, he wasn't primarily acting as your example but as your representative. In submitting to baptism, Jesus took his place with us.

Paul argued, "All of us who have been baptized into Christ Jesus were baptized into his death" (Rom. 6:3). But Jesus was baptized into death itself. His baptism by water was followed by an immersion in judgment and fire (Luke 12:49–50). As your representative and substitute, Jesus died the death you should have died. In being crucified, Jesus took your place. He received what you deserved so that you could receive what he first received from the Father.

Since you are united to Christ by the Spirit, and through faith, you are now "in Christ." And if you are in Christ, then what is true of Christ is also true of you. That's why Paul says that we have been "accepted in the Beloved" (Eph. 1:6 KJV). John Calvin draws out the dazzling connection:

> The title of Son truly and by nature belongs to Christ alone, yet He was revealed as Son of God in our flesh, that He who alone claimed Him as Father by right, could win Him for us also.... His fatherly love must flow to us in Christ. The best interpreter of the passage is Paul (Eph. 1: 6), where he says that we have obtained grace in the beloved, that we may be loved in God.[11]

Think on it! God now says of you what he said of Jesus in the river: "You are my beloved son. With you I am well pleased."

And as Jesus received the Spirit from the Father, so now do you. During his incarnation, Jesus was anointed by the Spirit and lived his entire life in total dependence on the Spirit. But following his resurrection and ascension, Jesus bequeathed the Spirit to his people, the church, so that we too can live in the Spirit's strength and power. Christ, who was baptized in water as your representative and in fire as your substitute, has now baptized you in his Spirit.[12]

And in the power of his Spirit, we now live *in* and *for* Christ.

3

With Jesus in the Desert: *Temptation*

> Therefore he had to be made like his brothers in every respect, so
> that he might become a merciful and faithful high priest in the
> service of God, to make propitiation for the sins of the people.
> For because he himself has suffered when tempted, he is able to
> help those who are being tempted.
>
> Hebrews 2:17–18

No one gets far in life without experiencing temptation. Parents will
often see the first hints of temptation even in their toddlers. Tell an
eighteen-month-old, "No, don't touch that." She stops. She looks
at you. She then slowly stretches out her hand, ever so close to the
forbidden object, and puts on her cutest smile.

Of course, it's not long before temptation becomes more serious
and sinister. Children are tempted to envy their siblings, steal toys,
and cheat in school. In a desire to fit in with their peers, teenagers are
tempted to compromise moral standards, pretend to be something
they are not, or treat others poorly. And as we grow older, the variety
and intensity of temptations increase.

The Scriptures speak often about temptation. In the Lord's
Prayer, Jesus teaches his disciples to pray, "Lead us not into
temptation, but deliver us from evil" (Matt. 6:13). When Jesus was

in the garden of Gethsemane on the night of his betrayal, he told his sluggish disciples to "Watch and pray that you may not enter into temptation" (Mark 14:38). The apostle Paul assures us, "No temptation has overtaken you that is not common to man. God is faithful, and he will not let you be tempted beyond your ability, but with the temptation he will also provide the way of escape, that you may be able to endure it" (1 Cor. 10:13). And the apostle James warns us not to blame God for temptation, "For God cannot be tempted with evil, and he himself tempts no one. But each person is tempted when he is lured and enticed by his own desire. Then desire when it has conceived gives birth to sin, and sin when it is fully grown brings forth death" (James 1:13–15).

But the gospel narratives give us far more than instruction about temptation and how to resist it. We see Jesus, the Son of God, anointed by and filled with God's Spirit, going behind enemy lines to stand against the Prince of Darkness himself. We get a front-row seat to one of the fiercest, most decisive battles ever waged in the cosmic war between heaven and hell.

Someone might wonder how this part of Jesus' history came to be recorded. There were, after all, no human witnesses to record it. Even if there had been, the temptations themselves were probably more internal than external: though the battle took place in the wilderness, we shouldn't imagine a devil in red tights facing off against Jesus. And while it is possible that Satan appeared to Jesus in physical form, the temptations were more likely of a visionary nature.[1] How, then, do we know what happened? The most reasonable answer is that Jesus himself told his disciples. Here's how the great Scottish preacher James Stewart imagined the experience taking root in Jesus' memory:

> Jesus told this story because the titanic struggle of the desert days and nights had marked his soul forever, and he could never forget. He could see and feel it after months as plainly as if it had happened only yesterday—the wild, desolate loneliness, the rocks and crags with the pitiless sun beating down on them by day and the biting night wind moaning across them in the dark, the prowling beasts,

the famishing hunger, the demon voices whispering to his heart, the grace of God and the angels that had brought him through. Jesus told his disciples of it because he could not help it. It would not hide.[2]

Let's journey with Jesus in the Judean desert and witness this face-off between the Christ and the Ancient Serpent. We will focus on Luke 4:1–13, with an eye on the battle itself, the conquering king, and the spoils of war—the fruits of his victory for us.

The Battle Itself

Luke sets the scene in Luke 4:1–2, "And Jesus, full of the Holy Spirit, returned from the Jordan and was led by the Spirit in the wilderness for forty days, being tempted by the devil. And he ate nothing during those days. And when they were ended, he was hungry." The place west of the Dead Sea is called the wilderness of Judea, but "desert" would be a better word. When Americans hear "wilderness," we tend to think of a pleasant mountain cabin in a national forest, not a rugged, desolate, barren terrain hostile to human dwelling. The Old Testament describes this same area as a "great and terrifying wilderness, with its fiery serpents and scorpions and thirsty ground where there was no water" (Deut. 8:15).

Jesus spent forty days in this harsh environment, steadily engaging an enemy whose ferocity matched the setting, whom Luke calls the devil (Luke 4:2), Matthew calls the tempter (Matt. 4:3), and Mark calls Satan (Mark 1:13). This is the serpent of Genesis 3, that great antagonist of humanity and of God himself. Now in the barren desert, the great adversary of God and Man aimed every cruel arrow in his deceitful quiver at Jesus, the baptized Son of God. Jesus was like Christian in Bunyan's *Pilgrim's Progress* when he faced Apollyon and was confronted with flaming "darts as thick as hail."[3]

The devil came to Jesus armed to the teeth but with a simple strategy of temptation. These temptations were both comprehensive and concentrated. On the one hand, Jesus suffered the full gamut of temptation. Luke 4:13 emphasizes this: "And when the devil had ended every temptation, he departed from him until an opportune time."

As the Scottish theologian Donald Macleod explains, "He endured the full force of temptation's ferocity, until hell slunk away, defeated and exhausted. Against us, a little temptation suffices. Against him, Satan found himself forced to push himself to his limits."[4] The gospel narratives thus affirm what we learn in Hebrews: "We do not have a high priest who is unable to sympathize with our weaknesses, but one who in every respect has been tempted as we are, yet without sin" (Heb. 4:15).

So Jesus experienced all temptation, but not in a generic way: the devil shaped these temptations for Jesus. Of course, they bore certain similarities with temptations anyone else might experience. For example, Jesus was tempted in regard to both bodily appetite (turn stones into bread) and ambition (worship Satan in exchange for the world's kingdoms). But these temptations were concentrated and specific to Jesus.

As any good angler knows, an effective lure must have both attractive bait and a sharp hook. The bait is necessary to the nature of temptation, for without an appeal, you wouldn't be tempted. But temptation to sin always includes a hook—that which makes the temptation dangerous and evil. We will understand Jesus' temptations better if we look at the bait and the hook as well as the defense in each challenge.

The First Temptation

The bait in the first temptation was satisfied hunger. It makes sense. Jesus had fasted for forty days and was hungry, so the devil said, "If you are the Son of God, command this stone to become bread" (Luke 4:3). What's the big deal? Why would it have been a sin for Jesus to turn stones into bread? After all, the time will soon come when Jesus will create bread from nothing (Mark 8:1–9). Why not turn stones into bread now?

Any hungry man wants the bait of food, but to bite this hook means Jesus would use his power in a way that would subvert his whole mission as incarnate man. As I. Howard Marshall wrote, "Jesus is being tempted to use his power as Son of God for his own ends instead of being obedient to the Father."[5] This temptation therefore strikes at a key element of Jesus' incarnation: his earthly dependence upon his heavenly Father.

Jesus does not falter, however. He parries this thrust from Satan with the mighty sword of the Spirit, the word of God. He quotes Deuteronomy 8:3, saying, "It is written, '*Man* shall not live by bread alone'" (Luke 4:4). Don't miss this: Jesus' answer reveals his humanity.[6] Jesus is being tempted as a *man*, and as a man he must resist. Satan wants to seduce the divine Son into bypassing the weakness and limitations inherent in his incarnate humanity. But Jesus resists, resolute in his refusal to grasp his equality with God, purposing instead to empty himself, take the form of a servant, and humble himself in true humanity by becoming obedient to the Father, even to the point of death (Phil. 2:5–8).

The Second Temptation

Despite the strength of Jesus' defense, the devil is not dissuaded from a second attack. Satan had not yet exhausted his arsenal, so he aimed a second flaming arrow at the heart of the Son. "And the devil took him up and showed him all the kingdoms of the world in a moment of time, and said to him, 'To you I will give all this authority and their glory, for it has been delivered to me, and I give it to whom I will'" (Luke 4:5–6).

This time, the bait is power: "all the kingdoms of the world." The devil shows him these kingdoms and says, "I can give you this." But these kingdoms were promised to Jesus already: "I will make the nations your heritage, and the ends of the earth your possession" (Ps. 2: 8). Had not God promised to Abraham a descendant through whom all the nations of the earth would be blessed (Gen. 12:1–3)? And wasn't Jesus, as the Son of Man, entitled to receive the kingdoms of the world from the Ancient of Days himself (Dan. 7)? In the end, this is exactly what will take place: "The kingdom of the world has become the kingdom of our Lord and of his Christ, and he shall reign forever and ever" (Rev. 11:15). The devil is baiting Jesus with his own inheritance.

There is a grain of truth in the devil's astounding claim in Luke 4:6, for he does enjoy some temporary authority over the earth.

The Scriptures describe Satan as "the god of this world" (2 Cor. 4:4) and "the ruler of this world" (John 12:31). As we read in 1 John 5:19, "The whole world lies in the power of the evil one." In some sense, the kingdoms of the world are in the devil's hand, under his authority.[7]

But because Satan desires (and thinks he deserves) complete and eternal authority, he doesn't bother hiding the hook in this temptation: "If you, then, will worship me, it will all be yours" (Luke 4:7). Now the evil is apparent. The devil has tempted Jesus to take a short cut in his mission and vocation. Why endure the Father's plan when you could skip the hard parts? Surely the end justifies the means! He could go ahead and seize the kingdom owed him—not by way of the cross, but through an act of treason against the Father.

Jesus, armed with God's Word, powerfully counters the attack. He begins the same way he did before: "It is written, 'You shall worship the Lord your God, and him only shall you serve'" (Luke 4:8). The Son of God will not be deterred from his mission. He will not be deceived by the devil's schemes. He will not accept a detour from the solitary road to Calvary. The kingdoms will be his, and they will come at the cost of his life, not the cost of his loyalty to and love for the Father.

The Third Temptation

The third temptation was the most insidious and enticing of all. Jesus has nailed his colors to the mast: he will be faithful to the Father. So the enemy changes the game and takes Jesus to the most sacred location on earth, the temple (Luke 4:9a). This was God's dwelling place, the site of his presence, protection, and favor. Here, the devil quotes the sacred book, using Scripture itself as his bait. "If you are the Son of God, throw yourself down from here, for it is written, 'He will command his angels concerning you, to guard you,' and 'On their hands they will bear you up, lest you strike your foot against a stone'" (vv. 9b–11). Did you catch how the tempter cleverly appeals to Jesus' declaration of allegiance to his Father? "If you trust God so much, then trust him to fulfill his word. Jump off here and prove that he'll do what he said he'll do."

But therein lay the hook: putting God to the test. Jesus is not deceived. As the true king of Israel, he knows God's law forwards and backwards. He will not be outwitted by the Bible-toting devil. He responds, "It is said, 'You shall not put the Lord your God to the test'" (v. 12). Jesus overcomes the enemy yet again, and Satan quits ... for now. When Luke notes that the devil plans to return at "an opportune time" (v. 13), he hints at what will come even through one of Jesus' disciples (see Luke 22:3–5).

The Conquering King

We have surveyed the battlefield and seen the outcome of this fierce contest between the devil and Jesus, but let's now zero in on Jesus as the conquering king. To grasp the full significance of Jesus' victory over Satan in this event, we must remember how the Old Testament foretold this great king. Several stories in particular form the backdrop to Jesus' temptation and reveal him as the new and true Israel, the second and "last" Adam.

Jesus: the New and True Israel

This story of Jesus' temptation should make us remember the story of Israel's temptations in the wilderness, following the exodus. Numerous features in the narrative point us in this direction. The forty days of Jesus' temptation (Luke 4:2) recall the forty years of Israel's wandering, but the specific temptations Jesus faced also parallel those faced by the new nation. "As was Israel, so Jesus is tempted by hunger (Ex. 16:1–8), tempted to worship something other than God (Ex. 32), and tempted to put God to the test (Ex. 17:1–3)."[8] And each passage Jesus quotes in response to the temptations comes from Deuteronomy (the first from 8:3, the second from 6:13, and the last from 6:16), the book that lays out God's law to Israel following the exodus. The specific passages Jesus quotes are directly connected to Israel's experience in the wilderness.

In those forty lonely desert days of testing, Jesus was reliving the story of Israel. He was facing the trials they had faced and failed. The people of Israel were the descendants of Abraham, called by God as a light to the nations. But when you read their history in the Old Testament, it soon becomes obvious that Israel was as capable of disobedience, wickedness, and idolatry as the rest of the nations. Israel failed in their vocation as the people of God. But now Jesus comes as Israel in person, the new and true Israel, the faithful remnant of God's people reduced to one man. And in each and every point where Israel had been defeated, Jesus conquers. Jesus obeys where Israel had disobeyed. Jesus triumphs where Israel had been vanquished. Jesus stands where Israel had fallen and failed.

Jesus: the Second and Last Adam

The story of Jesus' temptation should also make us remember the testing of Adam in the Garden of Eden, where the first head and representative of the human race had faced the enemy in the ideal conditions of paradise, yet lost. The first man fell, plunging all of humanity into sin and bringing the whole creation under the curse.

As we saw in the last chapter, Luke shared the genealogy of Jesus between the stories of Jesus' baptism and temptation. Unlike Matthew, Luke chose to trace Jesus' lineage not only to Abraham, but all the way back to "Enos, the son of Seth, the son of Adam, the son of God" (3:38), with the next verse saying, "And Jesus, full of the Holy Spirit, returned from the Jordan and was led by the Spirit in the wilderness" (4:1). Luke's point is clear: Jesus is the replacement for Adam.[9]

You may have heard of John Milton's epic poem *Paradise Lost*, which imaginatively retells the story of Adam and Eve's fall. Fewer readers know that Milton wrote another epic poem, a sequel to *Paradise Lost* called *Paradise Regained*. When I first heard about it, I thought it might be about the New Jerusalem, but it's actually about the temptation of Christ. Notably, Milton's poem is unbiblical in many details, but there are solid biblical grounds for the basic association between Jesus' victory over temptation and reversing the fall. For example, in Romans 5:12–21, Paul shows us how Adam's disobedience led to condemnation and death, while Christ's obedience led to justification and eternal life. And in 1 Corinthians 15:45–49, Paul writes that everyone bears the image of the first Adam, the man of dust, but we can also bear the image of the second Adam, the last Adam, the man of heaven.[10]

Irenaeus on Recapitulation

The greatest theologian in the second century was Irenaeus, the Bishop of Lyons and a disciple of Polycarp, the famed martyr of Smyrna who had known the apostle John. As an heir to the apostles, Irenaeus took up the mantle to guard the faith against the onslaught of false teachers. His five-volume work *Adversus Haereses* (*Against Heresies*) refuted the claims of the Gnostics, defended the early faith, and articulated his doctrine of "recapitulation."

Building on Paul's Adam-Christ typology (Rom. 5:12–21; 1 Cor. 15:21–22, 45–49), Irenaeus taught that Christ as the second Adam passed through every stage of human life in order to reverse Adam's sin and restore humanity to communion with God. Whereas Adam had fallen by eating the fruit of a tree, the second Adam restored us to God through death on a tree.

"When [the Son of God] became incarnate, and was made man, He commenced afresh the long line of human beings, and furnished us, in a brief, comprehensive manner, with salvation; so that what we had lost in Adam—namely, to be according to the image and likeness of God—that we might recover in Christ Jesus.

For as it was not possible that the man who once for all had been conquered, and who had been destroyed through disobedience, could reform himself, and obtain the prize of victory; and as it was impossible that he could attain to salvation who had fallen under the power of sin,— the Son effected both these things, being the Word of God, descending from the Father, becoming incarnate, stooping low, even to death, and consummating the arranged plan of our salvation....

For unless man had overcome the enemy of man, the enemy would not have been legitimately vanquished. And again: unless it had been God who had freely given salvation, we could never have possessed it securely. And unless man had been joined to God, he could never have become a partaker of incorruptibility.... God recapitulated in Himself the ancient formation of man, that He might kill sin, deprive death of its power, and vivify man; and therefore His works are true."[11]

This truth of Jesus as the second and last Adam has astounding implications for our faith. When I was a young believer, I always thought of Jesus' temptation in exemplary terms. That is, if Jesus was tempted in the desert by Satan and defeated these temptations by quoting the word of God, I needed to memorize lots of Scripture so that I could quote it when I felt tempted. That's true, as far as it goes. But it misses the deep significance of Jesus' temptation.

Jesus' temptations were not primarily exemplary. This story wasn't included to show us how to defeat temptation by being like him. Sure, there are lessons we can learn. But to focus on Jesus as an example misses the burden of the story. It misses the main point. For Jesus was tempted not mainly as our example but as our representative, our champion, the one who fights on our behalf, the one who triumphs in our place.

> What Adam had, and forfeited for all,
> Christ keepeth now, who cannot fail or fall.[12]

The good news in this story is that Jesus obeyed God and defeated temptation at every point where Israel, and Adam, and you and I have failed! Jesus was tempted as our brother, captain, and king. Adam, our first representative, was tempted in paradise and failed. Jesus, the second Adam and our final representative, was tempted in the desert and conquered. He reversed every aspect of the fall.[13]

What Jesus won in this initial victory was soon to be completed in his decisive victory on the cross and over the grave. Just as the young David, freshly anointed as Israel's king, assumed the role of champion and defeated Goliath on Israel's behalf, so Jesus, anointed by the Spirit in his baptism, assumed the role of our champion, to defeat and disarm the devil.[14]

The Spoils of War

When an ancient king won a battle on behalf of his people, he shared with them the plunder of the battle. His victory meant wealth for them. So it is with Christ. He has won the decisive battle against sin and Satan, and he shares with us the spoils of war.

The story of Jesus' temptation *does* have a very practical application, but it is different from what we might first expect. The application is not merely moral exhortation to resist or flee temptation, though Scripture does, of course, command us to both flee and resist. But the Scriptures do so much more. They provide us with rich and wonderful, gospel-laden, grace-infused, Spirit-inspired applications of Christ's priestly work to our lives.

For example, we learn in Hebrews 2 that Christ shared human nature with us. He was "made like his brothers in every respect" (v. 17). He "partook" of our same "flesh and blood" (v. 14), or had the same basic human nature that we have. As we saw in the first chapter of this book, the eternal Son united human nature to himself in the incarnation. And his union with us in nature becomes the foundation for our union with him in grace. His shared humanity with us equips him to be a "merciful and faithful high priest" (v. 17) who "suffered when tempted" and therefore "is able to help those who are being tempted" (v. 18).

Also, in Hebrews 4:14–16, we see that Jesus not only helps us but also sympathizes with our weaknesses because he "has been tempted as we are, yet without sin" (v. 15). When you are tempted, Jesus doesn't stand over you with condemnation and judgment. He stands beside you with understanding and compassion and readiness to give mercy and grace to help in time of need. Do you see what the writer to the Hebrews is doing? He is appealing to Christ's incarnation and priestly work in order to encourage tempted and suffering believers.

> O loving wisdom of our God!
> When all was sin and shame,
> A second Adam to the fight
> And to the rescue came.
>
> O wisest love! that flesh and blood
> Which did in Adam fail,
> Should strive afresh against the foe,
> Should strive and should prevail.[15]

Finally, we see also in Hebrews 4 that the same one who took our nature, endured temptation, and conquered it on our behalf has now ascended to God in human nature. Our great high priest "has passed through the heavens" (v. 14). He is at the right hand of God, interceding for us (Rom. 8:34). We will consider the significance of Christ's ascension in our nature in chapter 11, but for now, take heart in knowing that you have a brother on the throne.

4

With Jesus on the Mountain:
Transfiguration

And we all, with unveiled face, beholding the glory of the Lord,
are being transformed into the same image from one degree of
glory to another. For this comes from the Lord who is the Spirit.

2 Corinthians 3:18

In *The Abiding Presence*, Hugh Martin argues that when we read
the gospel narratives, we are not merely reading a biographical or
historical account of the life of Jesus but are *encountering Jesus himself.*
He bases this claim on the promise Jesus gives in Matthew 28:20,
"And behold, I am with you always, to the end of the age," a promise
fulfilled through the gift and ministry of the Holy Spirit (John 14:16–
26; 16:13–22). "The Spirit," writes Martin, "achieves Christ's presence
with his people."[1]

This means that when we read the stories about Jesus, we do not
simply interact with memories, stories, concepts, and ideas about
Christ, however true and precious these may be. No, we engage with
the Lord Jesus himself. When we see Christ in Scripture, we truly
behold him. And he, in turn, speaks to us.[2]

This insight gave me a fresh perspective on Christ's ministry to his people through his word and Spirit. It deepened my understanding of 2 Corinthians 3:18, "And we all, with unveiled face, beholding the glory of the Lord, are being transformed into the same image from one degree of glory to another. For this comes from the Lord who is the Spirit." The larger context of 2 Corinthians 3 is concerned with the veil covering the hearts of those who read Moses. This veil obstructed the Israelites' vision, preventing them from seeing God's glory, but it is removed for those who turn to the Lord Jesus. Therefore, when Christians read Scripture, we behold the glory of Christ. And in beholding his glory, we are transformed—changed into Christ's glorious image. The Spirit of the Lord makes all this happen.

Beholding Christ's glorious image is the key to spiritual transformation. In seeing Jesus, the Spirit of Jesus changes us. This dynamic of spiritual transformation is the epicenter of Christian discipleship and spiritual growth. And the Lord uses the gospel narratives themselves to accomplish this transformation. When we behold Christ in the apostolic record, we see his glory; when we see his glory, the Spirit works; when the Spirit works, we are changed.

This pattern is a helpful lens through which to read and study the next pivotal event in the life of Jesus: his transfiguration, recorded in Matthew 17:1–9, Mark 9:2–8, and Luke 9:28–36. Let's join Peter, James, and John as they stand with Jesus and behold his glory on the mountain. We will consider three transforming elements in this story: the vision of glory, the path to glory, and how we share in his glory.

The Vision of Glory

Luke tells us that the disciples "saw his glory" (v. 32) and provides details in the narrative describing the vision. The accoutrements of glory are everywhere. First there is the alteration in Jesus' face and clothing (v. 29). While Luke says that Jesus' appearance was "altered," Matthew and Mark use the more vivid word "transfigured" (Matt. 17:2; Mark 9:2), using the Greek verb *metamorphoō*, from which we get our word *metamorphosis*. This is the same word Paul uses for "being transformed" in 2 Corinthians 3:18, quoted above.[3] When John saw Jesus on the Isle of Patmos, "his face was like the sun shining in full strength" (Rev. 1:16). So the disciples beheld the resplendent radiance of Christ's majestic glory on that mountain. The bright light of Christ's glory also recalls Daniel 7:9, where the enthroned Ancient of Days is clothed in white. And in Psalm 104:1–2 we see God clothed in splendor and majesty, wearing light. So it is here: the glory of the divine nature shines from Jesus' face and emanates through his robes. The veil, for a brief moment, is lifted. His deity shines through his humanity. Thus Peter refers to this moment later as having been "eyewitnesses of his majesty" (2 Peter 1:16).

The disciples not only saw Jesus in his transfigured glory, they also saw two men talking to Jesus, "Moses and Elijah, who appeared in glory and spoke of his departure, which he was about to accomplish at Jerusalem" (Luke 9:30b–31). Strange. Why Moses and Elijah? They represent the law and the prophets, or so the traditional explanation goes. But the two Old Testament figures shared other similarities that we shouldn't miss. Moses and Elijah had each encountered God on Mount Sinai (Horeb, in the Elijah narratives). And both departed from this world in mystery. Moses was buried in a grave known only by God (Deut. 34:4–5), while Elijah was swept up to heaven in a chariot of fire, bypassing death altogether (2 Kings 2:11). Both Moses and Elijah were also important eschatological figures in Jewish thinking. Moses had been Israel's first prophet, and the Jewish people expected another prophet like Moses to come liberate Israel (Deut. 18:15; Acts 3:22). Some Jews also expected Elijah to return as the forerunner of the day of the Lord (Mal. 4:5). So while Moses and Elijah may represent the law and the prophets, their presence signals the arrival of the Messiah, thus affirming Jesus as the Christ.[4]

Next, notice their conversation topic: "And behold, two men were talking with him, Moses and Elijah, who appeared in glory and spoke of his *departure*, which he was about to accomplish at Jerusalem" (Luke 9:30–31). The word for "departure" is the Greek word *exodus*. As we've already seen, the gospel writers drew straight, bold lines between Israel's exodus from Egypt and Jesus. The exodus was the quintessential redemptive event in the Old Testament. It was the moment in history when God had stretched forth his mighty hand to deliver his people from oppression and slavery to make them a people for his own glory. But for the gospel writers, the first exodus foreshadowed the new exodus accomplished by Jesus. Jesus was the new Israel, the new Moses, who came to rescue his people from the slavery of sin and death.

What happens next is almost comical. Peter, James, and John had been asleep, and as soon as they wake up, Moses and Elijah begin to leave, so Peter says to Jesus, "Master, it is good that we are here. Let us make three tents, one for you and one for Moses and one for Elijah" (Luke 9: 33). The inclusion of Peter's faux pax serves at least two purposes. For one thing, it demonstrates the authenticity of the gospel record. Some liberal scholars argue that the transfiguration stories were inventions of the early church, not the record of actual events. But if they were invented, it's hard to see why the church would have made one of its key leaders look so ridiculous! The only conceivable reason for including Peter's gaffe is that it happened.

More importantly, Peter's statement tells us that the apostles immediately found the scene reminiscent of the exodus. They might have even expected the cloud that appears next (Luke 9:34). This mysterious cloud clearly alludes to the glory cloud (the *shekinah*) that led Israel in the wilderness, covered Mount Sinai, and filled the tabernacle (Ex. 13:21–22; 24:15–16; 40:34–38). Here again we have the trappings of glory in exodus imagery.

Then a voice speaks from the cloud. As at Jesus' baptism, the Father audibly affirms the Son: "This is my Son, my Chosen One; listen to him!" (Luke 9:35). Or, in Matthew's report: "This is my beloved Son, with whom I am well pleased; listen to him" (Matt. 17:5b). Both the transfiguration itself and the Father's glorious pronouncement must have infused the heart of Jesus with renewed strength for the arduous task before him. As James S. Stewart commented, "It was the assurance that God had a mighty stake in what was happening now upon the earth, and that behind the shadow and thundercloud and threatening tragedy stood power and love eternal, pledged to crown the soul of Christ with victory."[5] The Father's voice in that moment confirms Jesus' identity, teaching, and work. Jesus is God's Son, God's chosen one. And the alteration of his appearance previewed the glory to come.

The voice from heaven was also directed to the disciples, however. God the Father affirms the Son and enjoins the disciples to listen to him. They respond by falling flat on their faces in terror (Matt. 17:6). It reminds me of a scene in C. S. Lewis's novel *Prince Caspian*, when the cynical dwarf Trumpkin meets Aslan face to face. Trumpkin doesn't believe in Aslan—or in lions, for that matter. But when he finally meets Aslan and hears him speak in a voice, "with just a hint of roar in it," Trumpkin totters in trembling fear before him.[6] I think the disciples must have felt something like Trumpkin. Here is Jesus, the master they have walked with, listened to—and flatly contradicted on occasion. But now, for the first time, the veil is lifted and the full outshining of his radiance and glory overwhelms them. Dazzling white light, blinding to their eyes, too bright to behold, too stark and brilliant to gaze upon, and the voice of God descending from the heavens! Like Trumpkin at Aslan's roar, they tremble. They are terrified.

Maybe they remembered Moses' prayer from Exodus 33, one of the most daring prayers in all of Scripture: "Please show me your glory" (Ex. 33:18). Remember God's answer? "You cannot see my face, for man shall not see me and live" (v. 20). But then the Lord graciously made a way to grant the request in part (vv. 21–23). Perhaps Peter, James, and John recalled that event as they thought back through everything they had seen on the mountain. Moses had glimpsed only God's back, but the disciples gazed on the light of God's glory radiating from the face of Jesus Christ.

And they survived! They were not slain. They do not die. Why? Because in Jesus Christ, perfect deity and perfect humanity were joined together in a mysterious union. God had pitched his tent with man. In the end, Moses had the sweet memory of that glimpse of God's glory, but the disciples still had Jesus (v. 8). Moses and Elijah, law and prophet, had their place. But now Jesus was on the scene. His glory eclipsed all. God's final word is given in his Son.

The Path to Glory

This stunning vision of Christ's glory on the Mount of Transfiguration must have left the disciples stunned and amazed. But they were only beginning to learn the most painful and mysterious truth of all: that the path *to* glory leads *through* suffering.

We see this in how the transfiguration story is framed in the narrative itself. The sequence is very important. In all three accounts, the transfiguration comes directly after Peter's confession that Jesus was the Christ (Matt. 16:16: Mark 8:29; Luke 9:20) and Jesus' first prediction of his coming passion (Matt. 16:21; Mark 8:31; Luke 9:22), but shortly before his second prediction (Matt. 17:12; Mark 9:12; Luke 9:44). This ordering of events is not accidental.

Why was Jesus not transfigured at the beginning of his ministry, right after his baptism or temptation? Why were the disciples (and only three of them) given this vision of Christ's glory now? I think the reason is because they had finally begun to understand that Jesus' route to glory was through the suffering of the cross. Yes, Jesus had come to accomplish an exodus. But in this exodus, he would not only be Moses: *he would be the Passover Lamb, the one sacrificed to cover the sins of his people* (1 Cor. 5:7).

This theme runs through our study ... and indeed through the life of Jesus. The shadow of Calvary loomed over the Bethlehem manger. Jesus' baptism in the Jordan prefigured his baptism in the flood of God's fiery wrath. His temptation in the wilderness was the prelude to his final showdown with the powers of darkness in Gethsemane and on Golgotha. And the glory of his transfiguration previewed the glorious exaltation that would only follow his death on the cross.

Why is the path to glory marked by suffering? The writer to the Hebrews answers, "For it was fitting that he, for whom and by whom all things exist, in bringing many sons to glory, should make the founder of their salvation perfect through suffering" (Heb. 2:10). The path to glory is a path through suffering because the founder of our salvation will bring many sons to glory. He will not be glorified alone. Many will be glorified with him. But to do that, he must be made "perfect through suffering." Oswald Chambers explains,

If Jesus had gone to heaven from the Mount of Transfiguration, He would have gone alone; He would have been nothing more to us than a glorious Figure. But He turned His back on the glory, and came down from the Mount to identify Himself with fallen humanity.[7]

Jesus came down from the mountain to continue his journey toward another mountain—the mountain of crucifixion—so that he might lead his people to glory.

How We Share in His Glory

The disciples saw Jesus transfigured and then crucified before their very eyes. They may not have caught on as the events unfolded, but they soon understood—as we can also now—that Jesus' path to glory was marked by suffering. What seems less clear is how we get to share in his glory. How exactly does that work?

The Scriptures give us good warrant for asking this question. Paul describes Christians as those who "rejoice in hope of the glory of God" (Rom. 5:2c) and assures us that "When Christ who is [our] life appears, then [we] also will appear with him in glory" (Col. 3:4). God has called us to his kingdom and glory (1 Thess. 2:12). Jesus prayed that his people, given to him by the Father, would be with him to see his glory (John 17:24). Glory is our destiny, and it includes both future glorification and present transformation.

The future glorification will not be complete until the final resurrection, when our bodies will be raised in glory and power (1 Cor. 15:42–43) and transformed to be like the glorious body of Christ (Phil. 3:21). But glorification has already begun, for as we saw in the beginning of this chapter, the Spirit transforms us as we behold the glory of the Lord (2 Cor. 3:18). In fact, the word Paul uses for this process of transformation is the same word used by Matthew and Mark for Jesus' transfiguration.

How then are we transformed? How do we participate in the glory of Christ? The story of Jesus' transfiguration suggests that we must gaze on his face, listen to his voice, and walk in his steps.

Christ in All of Scripture

For many believers, reading the Old Testament is a daunting, dreary task. The records of patriarchs, priestly laws, and prophetic oracles of doom and judgment may hold some historic value, but frankly feel too far removed from real–life issues to hold our interest.

Maybe we're missing the point. Jesus claimed that the Old Testament Scriptures were about him (Luke 24:25–27, 44; John 5:39–40). And the best teachers of the church, for good reason, have always maintained that Jesus is the hero of every story of Scripture. Through regular reading and with the Holy Spirit as your guide, you too can develop the instincts for seeing Christ in all of Scripture. Watch as John Calvin does this kind of reading:

"When you hear that the gospel presents you Jesus Christ in whom all the promises and gifts of God have been accomplished; and when it declares that he was sent by the Father, has descended to the earth and spoken among men perfectly all that concerns our salvation, as it was foretold in the Law and to the Prophets—it ought to be most certain and obvious to you that the treasures of Paradise have been opened to you in the gospel; that the riches of God have been exhibited and eternal life itself revealed. For, this is eternal life; to know one, only true God, and Jesus Christ whom he has sent, whom he has established as the beginning, the middle, and the end of our salvation. He [Christ] is Isaac, the beloved Son of the Father who was offered as a sacrifice, but nevertheless did not succumb to the power of death. He is Jacob the watchful shepherd, who has such great care for the sheep which he guards. He is the good and compassionate brother Joseph, who in his glory was not ashamed to acknowledge his brothers, however lowly and abject their condition. He is the great sacrificer and bishop Melchizedek, who has offered an eternal sacrifice once for all. He is the sovereign lawgiver Moses, writing his law on the tables of our hearts by his Spirit. He is the faithful captain and guide Joshua, to lead us to the Promised Land. He is the victorious and noble king David, bringing by his hand all rebellious power to subjection. He is the magnificent and triumphant king Solomon, governing his kingdom in peace and prosperity. He is the strong and powerful Samson, who by his death has overwhelmed all his enemies....

This is what we should in short seek in the whole of Scripture: truly to know Jesus Christ, and the infinite riches that are comprised in him and are offered to us by him from God the Father. If one were to sift thoroughly the Law and the Prophets, he would not find a single word which would not draw and bring us to him. And for a fact, since all the treasures of wisdom and understanding are hidden in him, there is not the least question of having, or turning toward, another goal; not unless we would deliberately turn aside from the light of truth, to lose ourselves in the darkness of lies. Therefore, rightly does Saint Paul say in another passage that he would know nothing except Jesus Christ, and him crucified."[10]

Gaze on His Face

We know what happened during Jesus' transfiguration because the disciples saw it and were stunned (Matt. 17:2; Luke 9:32). As they gazed on the resplendent radiance of Jesus on the mountain, so we, by faith, gaze on the glory of God in Jesus (2 Cor. 3:18; 4:6). And we see that glory in the gospel.[8] We gaze upon Jesus' glory in the gospel and are "transformed by the renewal of [the] mind" (Rom. 12:2).

Gazing on God's glory by faith involves what Martin calls "a two-fold revelation"[9]—an *external* revelation of God's glory in the gospel and an *internal* revelation of this same glory to the soul by faith. Think of it like this: each person, spiritually, is like a blind man enclosed in a dark room. The man needs two things before he can see: sight and light. Sight gives him the faculty of seeing, while light illumines the object of his vision. In the same way, we need both the objective light of God's revelation and the internal illumination of the Holy Spirit.

Listen to His Voice

As the Father commanded the disciples to listen to the Son of his love (Luke 9:35), so he commands us to hear Jesus, to listen to Jesus, to pay attention to Jesus. This means that it is not enough to read the Bible. That is essential, but not enough. Do you remember what Jesus once said to a bunch of Bible experts? "You search the Scriptures because you think that in them you have eternal life; and it is they that bear witness about me, yet you refuse to come to me that you may have life" (John 5:39–40). It is possible to read the Bible and miss Jesus, so we must take care to see him and hear him. This may be one reason why Moses and Elijah appeared only briefly on the mountain: God was teaching the disciples to listen to the Son.[11]

Walk in His Steps

When Jesus first told his disciples about the suffering of the cross (Luke 9:22), he also taught them the first and most foundational lesson in discipleship: "If anyone would come after me, let him deny himself and take up his cross daily and follow me. For whoever would save his life will lose it, but whoever loses his life for my sake will save it" (Luke 9:23–24). The road to Calvary is the path to glory: this is the paradox of the kingdom. This pattern of suffering and glory, death and life, cross and resurrection runs through all of Scripture. The first is last and the last is first. To be great, you must be the servant of all. Brokenness is the condition of blessing. Humiliation is the pathway to exaltation. To live, you must die. The sure path to death is clinging to life. As Amy Carmichael wrote, "There is no gain except by loss, / There is no life except by death."[12]

This a lifelong process for the Christian, and it involves daily mortification. As Calvin observed, this mortification is both internal and external, involving crucifying the flesh and its lusts on one hand (Rom. 8:13; Gal. 5:24; Col. 3:5) and submitting to God's hand in the painful providences that attend this life on the other (John 15:2; 2 Cor. 4:7–12).[13] But mortification is only the means to the end. The suffering is temporary, leading to everlasting joy (see Heb. 12:2). After the cross comes the resurrection. After darkness, light.

The path is difficult, but it ends in glory.

5

With Jesus in the City: *Triumphal Entry*

Rejoice greatly, O daughter of Zion!
Shout aloud, O daughter of Jerusalem!
Behold, your king is coming to you;
 righteous and having salvation is he,
 humble and mounted on a donkey, on a colt, the foal of a donkey.

Zechariah 9:9

Jesus entered Jerusalem sometime before the annual Passover alongside other pilgrims journeying from Galilee to Jerusalem. With expectations high as they prepared to celebrate the festival, the pilgrims walked a long and steep road. The last leg began in Jericho, the lowest city on earth at about 800 feet below sea level, and ended 15 miles later in Jerusalem at nearly 3000 feet above sea level. The road passed through desert until you ascended the Mount of Olives. Then ... the first sight of the Holy City, a welcome relief after the arduous climb. There in Jerusalem was the temple, the place where the Lord God had pledged to reveal his presence to his people. The temple was the dwelling place of God, the place of daily sacrifice, the place where heaven met earth.

It is difficult to overstate the temple's importance. It was huge, filling about 25 percent of the city. Remember how on

September 11, 2001, terrorists hijacked four airplanes and attacked the World Trade Center and the Pentagon, unsuccessfully trying to attack either the White House or Capitol Hill as well? Imagine all those buildings rolled into one place—a place that is also the center of religious life in America—and you'll begin to grasp the monumental significance of the temple in Jerusalem. It carried the economic significance of the World Trade Center, the political significance of the White House or Capitol Hill, and the religious significance of a large national religious gathering place.[1]

So this is the scene. The pilgrims are making their way to Jerusalem, eager to reach the Holy City and the temple. They accompany Jesus. En route, outside Jericho, Jesus had healed a blind man who then called him "The Son of David" (Luke 18:35–43). Hopes are high. Electric excitement fills the air. And in this charged atmosphere, as he enters the city and then the temple, *Jesus acts*. What he does discloses more about his unique character and divine mission than perhaps any other single episode in his life prior to his passion.

As we also walk with Jesus into Jerusalem, we will contemplate four attributes he reveals on this journey: his authority, humility, compassion, and anger.

The Authority of Jesus

Jesus reveals his authority in the deliberate and detailed instructions he gives his disciples (Luke 19:28–31) and in the claims to kingship that his actions imply. Notice the details. Jesus instructs his disciples to go into the next village and conscript a colt for his use. Jesus does this to fulfill a specific prophecy, as we shall see in a moment. But his instructions also suggest his kingship, for in the Old Testament, kings had the right to enlist the use of a civilian's animal (1 Sam. 8:16–17).[2]

Jesus is actually called "king" in verse 38: "Blessed is the King who comes in the name of the Lord! Peace in heaven and glory in the highest!" The crowds are quoting Psalm 118, "a royal psalm recited on the annual enthronement of the king."[3] And when the Pharisees ask Jesus to rebuke them for saying this, he refuses, claiming that if they didn't say it, the rocks would (v. 40). Jesus is willing to accept his disciples' acclamations of praise and worship.

John's gospel describes the scene in more detail: "So they took branches of palm trees and went out to meet him, crying out, 'Hosanna! Blessed is he who comes in the name of the Lord, even the King of Israel!'" (John 12:13). These words and symbols show us that the people viewed Jesus as their king and deliverer. Typically used not during Passover but during the Feast of Tabernacles, palm branches had also become a national symbol for Israel during the Maccabean revolt two centuries before. So the crowds waved those branches in hopes that they would soon be liberated from the tyranny of Rome.[4] The Messianic overtones are clear.

Jesus demonstrates his kingly authority in the way he commands these events, intentionally entering Jerusalem and receiving both worship and exaltation as king. His actions were deliberate and symbolic, and they would have communicated a powerful message to his contemporaries. "Jesus in that tumultuous hour was issuing a challenge. Every token of royal honor which he accepted that day gave point to the challenge, and every hosanna of the crowd drove it home."[5] Thus, Jesus' royal ride into Jerusalem along with his subsequent words and deeds provoked the reigning powers.

The Humility of Jesus

Jesus' authority is different from that of earthly kings, for his authority is mingled with humility. As these events unfold, Jesus proves to be an entirely unique king: a servant king who establishes his reign through love and self-sacrifice. Notice the animal he chooses to ride—not a white charger, but a humble donkey. This obviously alludes to Zechariah's prophecy:

> Rejoice greatly, O daughter of Zion!
> Shout aloud, O daughter of Jerusalem!
> behold, your king is coming to you;
> righteous and having salvation is he,
> humble and mounted on a donkey,
> on a colt, the foal of a donkey.
>
> Zechariah 9:9

Luke's telling of the story doesn't emphasize this, but Matthew and John's do, and there can be no doubt that Jesus deliberately chose to enter Jerusalem this way. His actions were intentional, symbolic, and humble, especially in comparison to Roman triumphal processions. While Christians call this event the "triumphal entry," no Caesar or general of Rome would have thought it such, for they always returned to Rome after major military conquests in spectacular pageantry. The general would ride through the city in a golden chariot, with prisoners and spoils of war on display for all to see while priests burned incense in his honor. But Jesus was a different kind of king—a humble servant-king, riding a gentle, borrowed donkey.

This mingling of qualities in Jesus is utterly unique! The best comparison I have found is the medieval idea of chivalry, a paradox that C. S. Lewis said connected humility and courage, patience and intensity. The medieval knight, Lewis wrote, "is not a compromise or happy mean between ferocity and meekness; he is fierce to the nth and meek to the nth."[6] Similarly, the triumphal entry joins together two dissimilar attributes: Jesus' authority as Israel's true king and his humility as the servant of the Lord. As with Lewis's knight, in Jesus we see not a compromise between authority and humility, but complete authority *and* perfect humility. He is kingly lord to the nth and lowly servant to the nth. He is the servant-king, the kingly servant.

We see this paradox not only in what Jesus rides but also in *how* he rides. Note our Lord's matchless character. Jesus has all the authority of a king, but none of the arrogance, swagger, or pretension. He displays the humility of a true servant, but this in no way diminishes his majesty and glory. Jesus reveals his authority in humility.

As we reflect on Jesus' example, we should remember his words, "Truly, truly, I say to you, a servant is not greater than his master, nor is a messenger greater than the one who sent him" (John 13:16). If Jesus showed meekness even in his kingliness, how much more should we clothe ourselves in the garments of humility (Col. 3:12; 1 Peter 5:5)? When we become imperialistic, power-hungry, arrogant, or proud, we step away from the pattern of Jesus. Conformity to his image means adopting the humble mind of Christ and demonstrating

Christlike humility as managers and CEOs, parents and teachers, or pastors and elders.

The Compassion of Jesus

We might expect Jesus to now continue his procession to the temple, but he doesn't. What happens next reveals yet another dimension of Jesus' character: his tearful compassion.

> And when he drew near and saw the city, he wept over it, saying, "Would that you, even you, had known on this day the things that make for peace! But now they are hidden from your eyes. For the days will come upon you, when your enemies will set up a barricade around you and surround you and hem you in on every side and tear you down to the ground, you and your children within you. And they will not leave one stone upon another in you, because you did not know the time of your visitation."
>
> Luke 19:41–44

Jonathan Edwards on The Excellency of Christ

In a sermon on "The Excellency of Jesus Christ," Jonathan Edwards noted the "admirable conjunction of diverse excellencies in Jesus Christ" seen in Revelation 5, where Jesus is portrayed as both a lion and a lamb.

Edwards' sermon describes Jesus' infinite highness and infinite condescension, his infinite justice and grace, his infinite glory and lowest humility, his infinite majesty and transcendent meekness, his deepest reverence toward God and equality with God, his infinite worthiness of good alongside his greatest patience under sufferings of evil, his exceeding spirit of obedience alongside his supreme dominion over heaven and earth, his absolute sovereignty alongside his perfect resignation, and his self-sufficiency alongside his entire trust and reliance on God.[7]

Jesus' entry into Jerusalem displays a similar "conjunction of diverse excellencies" as we see humility joined with authority, and holy anger mingled with loving compassion. But, as Edwards observed in the third point of his sermon, the harmony of these attributes is nowhere more evident than at the cross, in Christ's "offering up himself a sacrifice for sinners."[8]

Why does Jesus weep? He considers the judgment that looms over them, a doom that would fall on the city in AD 70 as the Roman armies marched under their general and future emperor Titus to lay siege to Jerusalem and destroy the temple. Three times the Scriptures speak of Jesus' tears: at Lazarus' tomb in John 11, in Hebrews 5:7 as we read that Jesus "offered up prayers and supplications, with loud cries and tears" (no doubt referencing the anguish of Gethsemane), and here where the Savior weeps over Jerusalem. Jesus' tears show us his genuine humanity, revealing to us the depth of his human emotions. But they also reveal the heart of God, who is "not willing that any should perish but that all should come to repentance" (2 Peter 3:9b) (NKJV) and does not delight in the death of the wicked that they should die (Ezek. 18:23; 33:11).

Jesus' compassion is a rebuke to most of us. Our attitudes toward unbelievers are rarely marked by this kind of tender mercy. We usually feel indifferent, sometimes even condescending or malicious. But the example of Jesus teaches us that our disposition toward the lost should be one of heartfelt mercy and gentle compassion.

> Did Christ o'er sinners weep,
> And shall our cheeks be dry?
> Let floods of penitential grief
> Burst forth from every eye.
> The Son of God in tears
> The wondering angels see!
> Be thou astonished, O my soul,
> He shed those tears for thee.[9]

The Anger of Jesus

Finally, in the last paragraph, we see the righteous anger and judgment of Jesus. When Jesus comes to Jerusalem, he goes to the temple and does one of the most surprising things we see him do in the Gospels: he gets angry. "And he entered the temple and began to drive out those who sold, saying to them, 'It is written, "My house shall be a house of prayer," but you have made it a den of robbers'" (Luke 19:45–46). Mark tells us that Jesus even "overturned the tables of the money-changers and the seats of those who sold pigeons" (Mark 11:15).

The *Axis Mundi*

All of the great mythologies and religions of the world are concerned with the reuniting of heaven and earth. And many mythologies symbolize the connection between heaven and earth with a physical location—the *axis mundi*, or the center of the world. For example, the ancient Greeks believed that Mount Olympus was the home of the gods. Egypt had the pyramids, Mesopotamian civilizations their ziggurats, and some Native Americans their totem poles. The *axis mundi* has also found its way into modern architecture in symbols of secular power such as the Eiffel Tower and the Washington Monument. You even have something like an *axis mundi* in modern literature (consider, for example, the lamppost that unites our world with Narnia in *The Lion, the Witch, and the Wardrobe*).

But the original *axis mundi*, the first meeting place between heaven and earth, was the Tree of Life in the Garden of Eden. God designed the Garden as the center of creation, and he placed the first human beings there to live in perpetual fellowship with him. Of course, this fellowship was broken, this connection disrupted. Now we have heard the story of redemption God wrote about how he is reestablishing that broken connection.

In the Old Testament, Israel's *axis mundi* (though they didn't call it this) was wherever God revealed himself to his people—specifically Mount Sinai, the tabernacle, and then the temple. God promised that Israel would be his people and he would be their God. And in the face of Israel's disobedience, idolatry, and exile, the hope of the prophets was that a tree would come, a branch from the root of Jesse, a messianic king, who would restore Israel's fortunes and lead to a bright new age where God would once again dwell with his people.

The surprise of the gospel is that this connection has been made not in strength and power, but in weakness and shame. For the true *axis mundi*, the place where heaven and earth have met once and for all is the cross. This is what distinguishes Christianity from all other religions. In other religions, the *axis mundi* is the place where man reaches up for God: the place where sacrifices are made, prayers are offered, and the attention of the gods is sought. But in Christianity the *axis mundi* is the place where God reaches down for man. It is not the place where man sacrifices for God, but where God himself makes the supreme sacrifice. The cross is where heaven and earth are reconciled, where the alienation is overcome, where the mess is cleaned up, where *shalom* is restored.[10]

If Jesus' tears reveal the tenderness of his compassion, his anger exposes the zeal of his holiness. "Never did the volcanic element in the soul of Christ blaze out more terribly."[11] Yet this is the true Christ as well. The same eyes that brimmed with tears over perishing sinners, also burned in holy jealousy and zeal for his Father's glory. So we see more and more clearly the depth and complexity of Jesus' human emotions. We will consider more about Jesus' emotional life in the next chapter, but for now, it is important to see how Jesus' actions both pronounced judgment on the temple and invited judgment on himself.

Remember that the temple was designed as the dwelling place of God, the place of prayer and worship and sacrifice, but it had become a place for extorting the poor, and probably a tool for political power and corruption. We can infer this because the word "robbers" means "bandits" or "brigands" and was used of revolutionaries and Jewish nationalists whose hopes were set on military conquest. Jesus denounces this misuse of the temple and stands against the corruption and compromise. No wonder Jesus feels angry when he enters the temple. He finds not prayer, but merchandise; not worship and praise, but political agendas! So he quotes Jeremiah 7:11 and condemns this "den of robbers."

By driving the money changers from the temple, Jesus dramatically and symbolically announces the end of the sacrificial cult. Casting out those who trade in animals means a halt to sacrificial offerings. This would not have lasted for very long, of course, but as Wright observes, "The fact that Jesus effected only a brief cessation of sacrifice fits perfectly with the idea of a symbolic action. He was not attempting a reform; he was symbolizing judgment."[12]

Jesus' actions were not only revolutionary; they were provocative and incendiary. We can see the plot hatching in the malicious way that the temple leaders respond: they want to kill him but have a hard time figuring out how to do it because "all the people were hanging on his words" (Luke 19:48). Nevertheless, in a few days, their pregnant conspiracy will give birth to murder. Jesus' symbolic actions in the city lead directly to his crucifixion outside the city. By pronouncing judgment on the temple, Jesus invites judgment on himself. His stay in the city will end at the cross. And it is especially at the cross that we see the uniqueness of our Lord. Jesus may have entered Jerusalem as the servant-king, but he will exit Jerusalem as the shameful sacrifice.

Once again, we are confronted with the glorious paradox of the gospel. Because Jesus has all authority, he is not afraid to ride into Jerusalem as a king. Because Jesus is humble, he is not ashamed to ride in on a donkey. Because Jesus has deep compassion, he is not too proud to weep. And because Jesus will restore all things, he does not wince at displaying his anger in the house of prayer.

6

With Jesus in the Upper Room:
Farewell Discourse

> In that day you will know that I am in my Father, and you
> in me, and I in you.
>
> John 14:20

All Christians believe that "Christ Jesus came into the world to save sinners" (1 Tim. 1:15). Confessing our sins and our need for salvation are foundational to any meaningful profession of faith in Christ. As Paul says in Romans 10:13, "everyone who calls on the name of the Lord will be saved."

But what do we mean by the words save and salvation? Some people, when speaking about salvation, emphasize what happens in the life and heart of the sinner. Salvation is the experience of real transformation in one's soul that results in a changed life. It involves an internal work of regeneration or new birth, with faith in Jesus Christ and repentance from sin. In popular Christian jargon, it involves "accepting Christ" or "asking Jesus to live in my heart."

Others emphasize God's objective work through Jesus Christ for the redemption of sinners. From this perspective, salvation involves being rescued from Satan, sin, and death through the incarnation, crucifixion, and resurrection of the Son. The emphasis is not so much on what we do as on what God has already done for us in Christ.

Both of these perspectives are biblical. Some people, unfortunately, overemphasize one side or the other. Some people place all their emphasis on the necessity of personal transformation so as to eclipse the objective work of Christ on our behalf, while others so stress the objective and historic aspects that they lose sight of the need for personal faith in Christ and ongoing transformation. These two aspects of salvation—the objective and the subjective, the historic and the existential, what God has accomplished *for* us and what God now performs *in* us—need to be kept together.

And these two aspects enjoy glad wedlock in the doctrine of our union with Christ.[1] We have seen this doctrine as we have journeyed with Jesus, traveling first to the Bethlehem manger, through the river Jordan, across the Judean desert, to the Mount of Transfiguration, and into the city of Jerusalem. Throughout this book, we have read these narratives through the gospel lens of union with Christ because only when we are joined to Christ do we benefit from his saving accomplishments.

Perhaps you have wondered if Jesus himself ever spoke directly about our union with him. Maybe you even wonder whether we have read this doctrine into the gospel narratives!

In this chapter, we will listen to Jesus talk about this very truth. We will sit with the disciples in the upper room as Jesus delivers his final teaching to his disciples on the eve of his death. In this spacious chamber located on the upper level of a house in Jerusalem, Jesus ate the Passover meal with his disciples on the final evening before his arrest, trial, and crucifixion (Mark 14:15; Luke 22:12). And here he delivered the Upper Room Discourse (also called the Farewell Discourse, recorded in John 14–16), which is one of the richest passages in all of Scripture. This chapter will not cover all of Jesus' words from that night,[2] but we will focus on several places where Jesus teaches us about union with himself.

The Bond of this Union: The Spirit

Have you ever wished you could have been one of the twelve disciples? To have seen Jesus in the flesh? Imagine the privilege of walking and talking with Jesus for three years, of hearing him teach, of sitting down with him for meals. Imagine being an eyewitness to Jesus feeding the thousands, calming the storms, healing the diseased, and vanquishing the powers of darkness. Have you ever thought, "I wish I could have lived then, instead of now?" And yet, we have something even better! For Jesus told his disciples, "It is to your advantage that I go away, for if I do not go away, the Helper will not come to you. But if I go, I will send him to you" (John 16:7).

This "Helper," of course, is the Holy Spirit. The Greek word for Helper is *paraklētos*, and it appears only five times in the New Testament. Other versions of the Bible translate this as "Comforter" (KJV, NASB), "Advocate" (NET, NIV, NRSV), or "Counselor" (HCSB), for it carries the idea of one who comes alongside to offer aid, encouragement, and counsel.[3] Jesus refers to the Spirit as the *paraklētos* four times in the Farewell Discourse and says that the Spirit's ministry is so unique, beautiful, and powerful that receiving the Spirit is even better than Jesus' ongoing physical presence would have been. After all, the Spirit creates and secures our personal union with Christ. As Calvin said, "the Holy Spirit is the bond by which Christ effectually unites us to himself."[4]

In John 14:20, Jesus explains the Spirit's role in this. He says that on the day when you receive the Spirit of truth, "you will know that I am in my Father, and you in me, and I in you." So we come to know three things through the Spirit: (1) that Jesus is in the Father, (2) that we are in Jesus, and (3) that Jesus is in us. Apparently, the more we understand about the relationships between Father, Son, and Spirit, the more we understand our union in Christ.[5] This is what the church fathers referred to as *perichorēsis*, the inter-Trinitarian relationships of mutual love, joy, and delight. Look closely and you'll see in that word the roots of our English word "choreography." That's why C. S. Lewis described the Trinity in terms of a dance or drama.[6]

In the next verses, Jesus says more about how believers join this dance, and he makes an amazing promise that the Father and Son will make their home in our hearts (John 14:23). They do this through the indwelling of the Holy Spirit: "He dwells with you and will be in you" (v. 17). The indwelling of the Father and Son in our hearts is effected by the indwelling of the Spirit because he is both the Spirit *of the Father* (Matt. 10:20) and the Spirit *of the Son* (Gal. 4:6).[7] And it is the indwelling Spirit himself who binds us to Christ, thus effecting our union with him. As Ferguson writes, "Having the Spirit is the equivalent, indeed the very mode, of having the incarnate, obedient, crucified, resurrected, and exalted Christ indwelling us so that we are united to him as he is to the Father."[8]

So the Spirit is the bond of our union with Christ. He is also the Spirit of truth who leads us into all the riches deposited for us in Christ our treasury. We see this in John 16:13–15 as Jesus describes the role of the Spirit in leading us to Christ and glorifying Christ:

> When the Spirit of truth comes, he will guide you into all the truth, for he will not speak on his own authority, but whatever he hears he will speak, and he will declare to you the things that are to come. He will glorify me, for he will take what is mine and declare it to you. All that the Father has is mine; therefore I said that he will take what is mine and declare it to you.
>
> John 16:13–15

This important passage describes the ministry of the Spirit of truth and reveals the Trinitarian pattern of our communion with God. First, the Spirit of truth guides us into all truth. It is only and always through the truth of the Spirit-inspired apostolic word that the Spirit of truth now leads believers into the truth. Second, our communion with God in Christ has a Trinitarian shape. That is, we draw near to the Father through the Son, and we draw near to the Son through the Spirit.

One of the most formative theologians in my spiritual growth has been John Owen, a Puritan theologian I've already quoted more than once. Those familiar with Owen's work may think of him as the author of the famous trilogy on mortification, temptation, and indwelling sin. Owen's foremost concern, though, wasn't sin and sanctification as such, but communion and fellowship with the triune God. Owen thus made the following comment on these verses from John 16:

> These words show us how we can have communion with God. We cannot go directly on our own to the Father, nor does the Father deal directly with us. We can only approach the Father by Christ, for it is only by him we have access into the Father's presence.... But without the Holy Spirit's work, we cannot even come to the Father by Christ. As the things of the Father are deposited in Christ and brought to us by the Spirit, so the Holy Spirit teaches us how to pray and what to pray for. These prayers are, as it were, deposited with Christ, and Christ brings them to the Father.[9]

The gospel testifies to spiritual reality—a *reality with a profoundly Trinitarian shape*. And this Trinitarian reality is the pulsing heartbeat of grace. We're not merely students amassing information to be applied by willpower in our own strength. We are persons loved by our triune God and summoned into relationship with him—relationship initiated by the Father, effected through the Son, and secured in the Spirit. As Paul writes in Ephesians 2:18, "Through [Christ] we [all] have access in one Spirit to the Father."

The Picture of this Union: Abiding in the Vine

One of the most vivid and powerful illustrations for the believer's union with Christ in all of Scripture is that of the vine and branches.[10] Branches bear fruit only when they abide in the vine. So it is for believers: the only way we can glorify the Father with fruitful lives is by abiding in Jesus. This teaching is found in John 15, where Jesus continues to prepare his disciples for his imminent death and departure by instructing them about their calling and mission as his disciples, emphasizing their absolute dependence on him. As Jesus says in verse 5, "I am the vine; you are the branches. Whoever abides in me and I in him, he it is that bears much fruit, for apart from me you can do nothing."

Take some time to meditate on this magnificent metaphor:

- The *vine* is Jesus, while we (believers, disciples) are the *branches.*

- The Father is the *vinedresser* (v. 1)—that is, the gardener who tends the branches. He prunes the fruitful branches so they will bear more fruit (v. 2) and takes away the unfruitful branches, throwing them into the fire (vv. 2, 6).

- The *unfruitful branches* are nominal disciples: people who outwardly follow Jesus for a time, but fail to bear fruit. Remember the original context: Judas Iscariot has just left the upper room to betray Jesus.

- The *fruit* we are called to bear probably includes both the fruit of transformed character (similar to "the fruit of the Spirit" in Gal. 5:22–23) and the fruit of evangelism as we testify to Jesus and his work.

This much seems clear. The image of the vine and branches seems straightforward, though it offers great riches for meditation. But the illustration hinges on the word "abide," so we also need to understand that. What does it mean to abide? Who does it? How is it done?

What Does Abiding Mean?

Just as branches are connected to their vine, depend on their vine, and continue in their vine, so for believers to abide in Jesus implies connection, dependence, and continuance. Don't think of these as three successive steps but as three interwoven aspects of abiding.

Abiding in Jesus means enjoying union with him through a life-giving connection. The branch connects to the vine as the vine to the branch. The connection is mutual: we abide in him and he abides in us (John 15:4). It is what Paul describes as being "in Christ." No connection means no life, no fruit; connection means life and fruit.

Abiding in Jesus also means relying upon him as the life-giver. The branch depends on the vine, but the vine does not depend on the branch. The branch derives its life and power from the vine such that the branch is useless, lifeless, powerless without it. Thus, unlike connection, dependence is not reciprocal. Sap flows from the vine to the branch, supplying it with water, minerals, and nutrients that make it grow. And believers receive the "the vital sap of the Holy Spirit"[11] through our life-giving connection to Jesus. We are completely dependent upon Jesus for everything that counts as spiritual fruit (v. 4). Apart from him, we can do nothing (v. 5).

So abiding in Jesus means continuing to rely on him, remaining in him. In fact, the word for "abide" (*meno* in Greek) means to remain, stay, or continue. For example, in John 1:38–39, two of the disciples who first encountered Jesus asked him "Where are you *staying*?" They wanted to know where Jesus made his residence. The word "staying" is the same word translated "abide" in John 15. To abide is to reside and remain in Jesus. We go on trusting, we keep on depending, we never stop believing. Abiding in Jesus means persevering in Jesus and his teaching. "If you abide in my word," he said, "you are truly my disciples, and you will know the truth, and the truth will set you free" (John 8:31–32).

Who Abides?

Jesus' description of abiding seems like an all or nothing deal. Abiding in him and his love and his word proves you are his disciple, whereas not abiding in him and his love and word shows that you are not a disciple at all. That's why John writes of abiding in such categorical terms: "Whoever confesses that Jesus is the Son of God, God abides in him, and he in God" (1 John 4:15) and "Everyone who goes on ahead and does not abide in the teaching of Christ, does not have God. Whoever abides in the teaching has both the Father and the Son" (2 John 9). To be a believer is to abide.

At the same time, we must recognize that Jesus commands us to "abide" (John 15:4). He tells us to abide in him and in his love (v. 9). It's something we are, but it's also something we must do.

Certain streams of Christian teaching have made this unnecessarily complicated. They have suggested that abiding in Christ is something additional that we gain through a crisis experience ushering into a higher, deeper, or victorious life. Sometimes this is even called the "abiding" life. Christians can therefore be broken down into two groups: the haves and have-nots, the ordinary Christians who believe in Jesus but don't abide and the extraordinary Christians who believe but also abide.

A simpler and closer reading of the text suggests that abiding, like faith itself, is a reality true of all Christians *and* an experience that we grow into by degrees. It's not that some Christians abide and some don't. If you believe in Jesus, you are in him! You enjoy union with him. You are connected to the life-giving branch. But no matter where you are on your spiritual journey, you can experience the reality of this connection to Jesus more and more. You can become more fruitful. After all, the passage not only speaks of bearing fruit, but also of bearing "more fruit" (v. 2) and "much fruit" (v. 8). You can enjoy Jesus more ... with joy, yes, but even *full* joy (v. 11). You can be more like Jesus. You can experience the sweetness and power of your connection to him more as you grow more dependent on him. In theological terms, all believers have union with Christ, but all believers can also experience communion with Christ in greater (or lesser) degrees.

How Do You Abide?

If abiding in Jesus involves ongoing daily dependence on him, what does that look like? Jesus himself tells us: we abide in Jesus by letting his words abide in us (v. 7) and by abiding in his love (vv. 9–10). To put it simply, abiding in Jesus does not mean advancing beyond the gospel to something else. It doesn't demand a crisis decision or a mystical experience. It just means keeping the words of Jesus in our hearts and minds so that they are renewing and reviving us, shaping and sanctifying us, filling and forming us. And it means keeping ourselves in his infinite, enduring, sin-bearing, heart-conquering, life-giving love.

John Owen described abiding in Christ in a whole-souled way involving our minds, wills, and affections. We use our minds to think about him, we exert our will in careful obedience to him, and we cultivate our affections to love him and to love what he loves more and more.[12] Our role is to remain in Christ, the true vine, and Jesus gives us all the tools we need to do just that. While we have a clear responsibility to abide, the security of our union with Jesus doesn't depend on what we do but on him. Jesus commands us to abide in him and then prays without ceasing for us.

The Security of this Union: The Intercession of Christ

John 17 gives us the longest prayer of Jesus recorded in Scripture. Throughout this prayer, Jesus reveals his unswerving commitment to both the glory of the Father and the good of his people.[13] This prayer therefore shows us what our union with Christ means to Christ himself.

In verse 2, Jesus identifies his people with the first of several words or phrases used throughout his prayer: he has been *given* these people, and he will *keep, sanctify,* and *glorify* them. Let's consider these words and phrases more closely to see how they highlight the unshakeable security of our union with Christ. Think of these words as links in what the Puritans once called the "golden chain of salvation."

Given

The first link in this chain is election, for Jesus' prayer shows us how God's people are *given* by the Father to the Son.

- Verse 2: "You have given him authority over all flesh, to give eternal life to all whom you have *given* him."
- Verse 6: "I have manifested your name to the people whom you *gave* me out of the world. Yours they were, and you *gave* them to me, and they have kept your word."
- Verses 9–12a: "I am praying for them. I am not praying for the world but for those whom you have *given* me, for they are yours. All mine are yours, and yours are mine, and I am glorified in them. And I am no longer in the world, but they are in the world, and I am coming to you. Holy Father, keep them in your name, which you have *given* me, that they may be one, even as we are one. While I was with them, I kept them in your name, which you have *given* me."
- Verse 24: "Father, I desire that they also, whom you have *given* me, may be with me where I am, to see my glory that you have given me because you loved me before the foundation of the world."

Christ's disciples are those given to him, entrusted to his care and keeping as a divine love-gift from the Father. Paul described the same reality in language we use more commonly—the language of choosing and electing (cf. Eph. 1:4; Col. 3:12; 1 Thess. 1:4). And both Paul and John understood that those given or chosen or elected would most certainly remain in Christ forever. When Jesus prays about those given to him in John 17, we would do well to remember John 6:37 and 10:27–29 where Jesus said that all those the Father had given to him would come to him and never be snatched away. Why? Jesus says it's because he and the Father are one (John 10:30). We are secure in the purposes of God.

Kept

When Jesus prays for the sheep that the Father have given him, he asks that they may be *kept*. This is the second link. Jesus himself has kept them up to this point, but as he moves toward the cross, he now entrusts them to the Father's strong hands.

> Holy Father, keep them in your name, which you have given me, that they may be one, even as we are one. While I was with them, I kept them in your name, which you have given me. I have guarded them, and not one of them has been lost except the son of destruction, that the Scripture might be fulfilled.... I do not ask that you take them out of the world, but that you keep them from the evil one.
>
> John 17:11b–12, 15

It is a stunning truth that none given to Jesus will ever be lost. The believer rests securely in the Father forever.

Sanctified

In verses 17 and 19 of John 17, Jesus prays that his people will be *sanctified*: "Sanctify them by the truth; your word is truth" and "For their sake I consecrate myself, that they also may be sanctified in truth." Jesus' prayer thus teaches us two important things about sanctification. First, God's Word is the means by which we are cleansed, washed, and made holy (cf. Eph. 5:26–27). Second, we are sanctified in union with Christ himself. In fact, the word for "consecrate" in verse 19 is *hagiazō*, translated "sanctify" in the NIV. This clarifies the connection between Christ's sanctification of himself in his work and his prayer for the sanctification of his people. *Our sanctification is in Christ.* As Paul says in 1 Corinthians 1:30, Christ is not only our redemption and righteousness, but also our sanctification.[15]

The Gospel Mystery of Sanctification

Walter Marshall was a Puritan pastor with a sin problem. Despite his best efforts, he just couldn't seem to come out as victor in his many skirmishes with the lusts of the flesh. He read the practical manuals on sin and holiness written by his fellow Puritan pastors, but they didn't provide much relief.

Marshall finally found help from Thomas Goodwin, a well-known pastor from whom he sought counsel. After Marshall confessed his many sins, Goodwin told him he had left out the greatest sin of all: unbelief. Then Goodwin pointed him to Christ. As Marshall started focusing on Christ and his fullness, his life and ministry began to change. Years later he penned these words in *The Gospel Mystery of Sanctification*:

"One great mystery is that the holy frame and disposition, by which our souls are furnished and enabled for immediate practice of the law, must be obtained by receiving it out of Christ's fullness, as a thing already prepared and brought to an existence for us in Christ and treasured up in Him; and that as we are justified by a righteousness wrought out in Christ and imputed to us, so we are sanctified by such a holy frame and qualifications as are first wrought out and completed in Christ for us, and then imparted to us.... So that we are not at all to work together with Christ, in making or producing that holy frame in us, but only to take it to ourselves, and use it in our holy practice, as ready made to our hands. Thus we have fellowship with Christ in receiving that holy frame of spirit that was originally in Him.... This mystery is so great that notwithstanding all the light of the gospel, we commonly think that we must get a holy frame by producing it anew in ourselves and by forming and working it out of our own hearts. Therefore many that are seriously devout take a great deal of pains to mortify their corrupt nature and beget a holy frame of heart in themselves by striving earnestly to master their sinful lusts, and by pressing vehemently on their hearts many motives to godliness, laboring importunately to squeeze good qualifications out of them, as oil out of a flint. They account that, though they may be justified by a righteousness wrought out by Christ, yet they must be sanctified by a holiness wrought out of themselves."[14]

Glorified

The fourth link in this golden chain takes us back full circle to the beginning of Jesus' prayer. As we saw above, glorification is a running theme in Jesus' prayer. He prays both for the Son to be glorified by the Father and for the Father to be glorified in the Son (John 17:1–5). But this mutual glorification of Father and Son is not unrelated to the disciples' good, for Jesus says that he will be "glorified in them" (v. 10). We are not only sanctified in Christ, but we are also glorified in him.

Jesus returns to this reality as he concludes his intercession. These requests stretch our imaginations to the limit:

> I do not ask for these only, but also for those who will believe in me through their word, that they may all be one, just as you, Father, are in me, and I in you, that they also may be in us, so that the world may believe that you have sent me. The glory that you have given me I have given to them, that they may be one even as we are one, I in them and you in me, that they may become perfectly one, so that the world may know that you sent me and loved them even as you loved me. Father, I desire that they also, whom you have given me, may be with me where I am, to see my glory that you have given me because you loved me before the foundation of the world.
>
> John 17: 20–24

What wondrous love is this! Jesus prays for the highest experience of union and communion that human beings can enjoy: he wants us, lowly mortals that we are, to be pulled further up and further in to the overflowing joy and everlasting love of the triune God himself. He wants us to experience the uppermost pinnacle of pleasure, the greatest summit of surpassing satisfaction—to be *with* Christ, to be *in* the Father and the Son, and to behold with unfading vision the resplendent glory of the eternal Son.

Here is love too wide for comprehension, beauty too deep for words, and joy too broad for song. But how will this prayer be fulfilled? *And at what cost?* We will answer these questions in the next three chapters as we journey with Jesus to Gethsemane, to Jerusalem's courtrooms, and then, to Golgotha.

7

With Jesus in the Garden: *Gethsemane*

In the days of his flesh, Jesus offered up prayers and
supplications, with loud cries and tears, to him who was able to
save him from death, and he was heard because of his reverence.
Although he was a son, he learned obedience through what
he suffered.

Hebrews 5:7–8

J. R. R. Tolkien's *The Children of Hurin* is one of the saddest stories
I've ever read. Tolkien's story combines the tragedies of a thwarted
lover, a wrongly accused and exiled man, a defeated warrior, and
a child separated from his parents, all culminating in a riveting
but devastating finale. But sad as this story is, the sorrows of
these characters were fictional. Their grief was far less than that of
Jesus, the Man of Sorrows, who faced the most piercing sadness in
Gethsemane's garden on the night of his betrayal.

The garden, like nowhere else, opens a window into the fully
human emotional life of the Lord Jesus.[1] In that olive grove, we see
the sinless Son of Man alone and afraid, wrestling with anguish as
he considers his impending death, for the sorrows of the garden are
closely tied to the cross.[2] That night in Gethsemane, the Son talks

with his Father about what it will take to save his people, and it throws him into great agony. His prayer also reveals the depth of his desire and determination.

The Savior's Anguish

The evidence of our Lord's anguish that night spreads over the entire narrative—in his emotions, words, and actions. Consider just the opening verses of Mark's version:

> And they went to a place called Gethsemane. And he said to his disciples, "Sit here while I pray." And he took with him Peter and James and John, and began to be greatly distressed and troubled. And he said to them, "My soul is very sorrowful, even to death. Remain here and watch."
>
> Mark 14:32–34

Notice the language used to describe Jesus' emotions. First, he is "greatly distressed and troubled" (v. 33). As Garland notes, the word for "greatly distressed" suggests "the greatest possible degree of horror and suffering."[3] Jesus was in mental and emotional anguish. He felt deeply anxious. Add to this his deep sadness: "My soul is very sorrowful, even to death" (v. 34).

The depth of Jesus' grief is also evident in his posture in verse 35: "And going a little farther, he fell on the ground and prayed that, if it were possible, the hour might pass from him." According to Ferguson, it was "a very unJewish thing" to fall prostrate on the ground in prayer.[4] Neither stoic nor proper, Jesus embodies his grief in a desperate physical display of lament.

Luke, the beloved physician, provides a further detail: "And being in an agony he prayed more earnestly; and his sweat became like great drops of blood falling down to the ground" (Luke 22:44). The sweating of blood is a rare medical condition called hematidrosis, which can be induced by extreme stress. Blood vessels around the sweat glands rupture, and the sweat glands then release congealed blood, giving the appearance of sweating blood.[5] Our Lord truly carried a great burden to prayer that night.

The Emotions of Jesus

Ever since the church's infancy, some people have been too "spiritual" to accept the real humanity of Jesus (1 John 4:1–3; 2 John 7). The Docetists said that Jesus only appeared to have a human body (the Greek word *dokeo* means "to appear"). He was essentially God in a man-suit. The Apollinarians believed that Jesus had a human body, but a divine soul. Against these and other distortions, Scripture portrays Jesus in all the living color of his genuine humanity—including his emotions.

In his seminal essay on "The Emotional Life of our Lord," B. B. Warfield surveyed the emotions attributed to Jesus in Scripture. He found that though Jesus was never ruled by his emotions, he certainly showed a full range of them:

- Compassion (Matt. 9:36; 14:14; 15:32; 20:34; Mark 1:41; 6:34; 8:2; Luke 7:13)
- Love (Mark 10:21; John 13:1, 34; 14:21, 31; 15:8–13)
- Anger (Mark 3:1–6; 10:13–14; 11:15–19; John 2:13–17; 11:33, 38)
- Sorrow (Isa. 53:3–4; Matt. 26:38; Mark 14:34)
- Gladness and joy (Luke 10:21; Heb. 12:2)
- Perplexity (John 12:27; 11:33; 13:21)
- Wonder (Matt. 8:10; Luke 7:9) and Desire (Luke 22:15)

Warfield concluded his study thus: "Not only do we read that he wept (John 11: 35) and wailed (Luke 19:41), sighed (Mark 7:34) and groaned (Mark 8:12); but we read also of his angry glare (Mark 3:5), his annoyed speech (Mark 10:14), his chiding words (e.g. Mark 3:12), the outbreaking ebullition of his rage (e.g. John 11:33, 38); of the agitation of his bearing when under strong feeling (John 11:35), the open exultation of his joy (Luke 10:21), the unrest of his movements in the face of anticipated evils (Matt. 27:37), the loud cry which was wrung from him in his moment of desolation (Matt. 27:46). Nothing is lacking to make the impression strong that we have before us in Jesus a human being like ourselves....

Various as [the emotions] are, they do not inhibit one another; compassion and indignation rise together in his soul; joy and sorrow meet in his heart and kiss each other. Strong as they are—not mere joy but exultation, not mere irritated annoyance but raging indignation, not mere passing pity but the deepest movements of compassion and love, not mere surface distress but an exceeding sorrow even unto death,— they never overmaster him. He remains ever in control."[6]

Jesus' distress was further heightened by his friends' failures right when he needed them most. Three times Jesus leaves the disciples to watch and pray. Three times he returns to find them sleeping (Mark 14:37–41). And when Jesus is finally betrayed and arrested, what do they do? "They all left him and fled" (v. 50). Earlier that night, each one of the disciples had pledged to die with Jesus (v. 31). Now, they each run from the scene of danger. Before the night finishes, Peter will fail Jesus further, denying him three times, ultimately with a curse.

Verses 51–52 refer to yet another figure, a young man who becomes "the first recorded streaker in history."[7] Who was this and why did Mark recount his flight? It could be an echo of Amos 2:16, where the prophet says that on the day of the Lord, "Even the bravest warriors will flee naked" (NIV). N. T. Wright sees an allusion to the garden of Eden: "Like Adam and Eve, the disciples are metaphorically, and in this case, literally, hiding their naked shame in the garden."[8] But since this incident is found only in Mark's gospel, many interpreters believe the young man was John Mark himself, who makes this appearance in his own narrative much as a film director might make a quiet cameo in one of his films. Whoever the figure is, he flees as well, leaving the Lord Jesus to face his accusers alone.

So here is Jesus forsaken, abandoned. Frederick Knowles captured the utter solitude of Jesus' suffering and distress in his poem "Grief and Joy":

> Joy is a partnership,
> Grief weeps alone;
> Many guests had Cana,
> Gethsemane had one.[9]

Jesus' earthly ministry began at a wedding and ended weeping. What started with miraculous winemaking finished with miraculous ear-healing. Everyone left the first scene happy, even though few knew what had happened. Everyone left the last scene with some sense of what had happened, yet feeling angry, confused, or sad. Jesus alone knew the weight of it all.

Jesus' anguish in the garden teaches us two important things. First, the sighs, groans, and tears of the Savior provide us with the strongest possible evidence of his full and complete humanity. Jesus was not merely God in a man-suit. Ours is not a Docetic

Christology, where Jesus only appeared to take human nature. No, he was "complete in divinity and complete in manhood, truly God and truly man, consisting also of a rational soul and body."[10] This means not only that he had a true flesh-blood-and-bone human body, but also that he had fully human faculties and emotions. He was "made like his brothers *in every respect*" (Heb. 2:17) and "*in every respect* has been tempted as we are, yet without sin*" (Heb. 4:15). His human nature was as truly human as yours. His emotions were every bit as real, his feelings just as acute, his sorrow and anxiety and fear as painfully palpable as yours. He "[took] upon Him man's nature, with all the essential properties and common infirmities thereof, yet without sin."[11] He was (and is) one of us: very man of very man.

We also learn from Jesus' anguish in the garden the importance of honestly expressing our emotions. Religious people sometimes think and act as if the open communication of emotion is dangerous, unspiritual, and wrong. We tend to stuff emotions, or mask them, or pretend they are not there. Jesus did not. He was "a man of sorrows and acquainted with grief" (Isa. 53:3), and his sorrows were not covered, repressed, or denied. Jesus is the perfect human being. Like the Hebrew poets of the Old Testament who left us their tear-stained psalms of lament, so Jesus models the need to face our feelings with honesty.

The Savior's Prayer

Why did Jesus suffer emotionally as he did? We get an insight into this in Jesus' prayer in the garden: "And going a little farther, he fell on the ground and prayed that, if it were possible, the hour might pass from him. And he said, 'Abba, Father, all things are possible for you. Remove this cup from me. Yet not what I will, but what you will'" (Mark 14:35–36). There are two parts to this prayer: request and submission.

The Request: "Remove This Cup from Me"

Jesus expressed his request with full confidence in his all-powerful and all-loving Father, for whom all things are possible. "Remove this cup from me," he pleaded.

What was this cup? In the Old Testament, the cup was a metaphor for God's judgment and wrath. The prophet Isaiah, for example, said:

> Wake yourself, wake yourself,
> stand up, O Jerusalem,
> you who have drunk from the hand of the Lord
> the cup of his wrath,
> who have drunk to the dregs
> the bowl, the cup of staggering.
>
> Isaiah 51:17

Consider also Psalm 11:6, which says the cup of the wicked will be full of "fire and sulfur and a scorching wind." Ezekiel speaks of a "cup of horror and desolation" (Ezek. 23:33). And in Revelation, we read of "the cup of the wine of the fury of [God's] wrath" (Rev. 16:19). This cup holds nothing short of God's fury against human sin and rebellion.

Jesus was about to drink that cup—the cup of God's wrath and judgment against sin. Not God's fury against Jesus' sins, for he was sinless, but God's fury against the sins of people made his own through imputation. Paul, in fact, will go so far as to say Jesus was made sin for us (2 Cor. 5:21). And this is why he shrank from it in such horror. "He was to drink the cup of curse and condemnation," said the Scottish theologian known as "Rabbi" John Duncan. "He did not leave one bitter drop for us, but drank it to the dregs; and instead, he put into our hands the cup of salvation."[12]

Nothing in all of history or literature can help us fully grasp how the imputation of our sins to the holy Son of God filled his soul with sorrow. No comparison would be just. But, following Hugh Martin, we can imagine Christ's sorrows by considering the contrasting joys of imputed righteousness. Think of the inexpressible and glorious joy that belongs to those whose sins are forgiven, whose consciences are cleansed, whose nakedness is covered in the spotless robe of Christ's righteousness! Drink in the gladness of forgiven sinners, now adopted into God's family and given bold access to his holy throne!

Then reverse it.

What must be the sorrow of the one who, though he knew no sin, is made sin for us? What must be the soul-anguish of the Son of God—the one holy, harmless, and "separated from sinners" (Heb. 7:26), yet now judged guilty, condemned by the divine Judge and cursed by the holy law? The simple fact that Jesus asked his Father to remove the cup from him explains the depth of his anguish. His dismay at this cup was not merely the dark dread of death. It was the consternation of one about to consume the cup of divine wrath and condemnation. It was the bewilderment of one who would bear the dreadful curse on behalf of his wayward, beloved bride. In the words of William Lane:

> The dreadful sorrow and anxiety, then, out of which the prayer for the passing of the cup springs, is not an expression of fear before a dark destiny, nor a shrinking from the prospect of physical suffering and death. It is rather the horror of the one who lives wholly for the Father at the prospect of the alienation from God which is entailed in the judgment upon sin which Jesus assumes.... Jesus came to be with the Father for an interlude before his betrayal, but found hell rather than heaven opened before him, and he staggered.[13]

The Submission: "Yet Not What I Will, but What You Will"

Jesus' request, so earnestly felt and fervently expressed to the Father, was coupled with submission. For Jesus also prayed, "Yet not what I will, but what you will" (Mark 14:36). Or in the slightly different wording found in Luke, "Nevertheless, not my will, but yours, be done" (Luke 22:42b).

This submission was consistent with and necessary to the obedience Jesus had practiced his entire life. Jesus' earliest recorded words expressed his desire to be about his Father's business (Luke 2:49). Throughout his life and ministry, his food was to do his Father's will and accomplish the work for which his Father had sent him (John 4:34). Jesus' singular ambition, throughout his life, was to fully and joyfully obey the Father's will. And so it was now.

Jesus' prayer of submission therefore shows the absolute necessity of the cross for salvation. Jesus asked the Father to remove the cup if possible, but it was not. Only in this way could God's holy love be reconciled with divine justice. This lonely road of humiliation, obedience, and death—even death on the cross—was the solitary path to the redemption of God's people. As the writer to the Hebrews says:

> Consequently, when Christ came into the world, he said,
> "Sacrifices and offerings you have not desired,
> but a body have you prepared for me;
> in burnt offerings and sin offerings
> you have taken no pleasure.
> Then I said, 'Behold, I have come to do your will, O God,
> as it is written of me in the scroll of the book.'"
>
> Hebrews 10:5–7

So does the Father answer the Son's prayer that night in the garden? Or is it the supreme example of unanswered prayer? Just as we draw comfort in our grief from reflecting on the Savior's sorrows, it may seem a strangely comforting prospect to think that Jesus has also experienced the disappointment of unanswered prayer—like we sometimes do. And it is true that the Father denied his first request to have the cup pass. But it would be wrong to say that the Father did not hear or answer the Son's prayers in the garden. We know this because Hebrews 5:7 tells us that "In the days of his flesh, Jesus offered up prayers and supplications, with loud cries and tears, to him who was able to save him from death, *and he was heard because of his reverence.*"

The Father heard the Son and answered him. No, the cup did not pass; it was not possible that it should pass. But Jesus was heard, God's will was done, and the Son "received all needful grace, all sustaining strength, qualifying and enabling Him to endure the cross and despise the shame; and gain an eternal title to the joy that was set before him."[14] Far from being a memorial to unanswered prayer, Gethsemane stands as an everlasting monument to the faithfulness of both the Father and his Son.

The Savior's Obedience

Having submitted to the Father his sinless reluctance to drink this cup of suffering and shame, Jesus returns to his sleeping disciples and announces, "the hour has come" (Mark 14:41).

He makes no attempt to escape. The redemptive plan, conceived in the eternal counsel of God and ratified in the covenant between the Father, Son, and Spirit must and will be carried out. This is the path Jesus will tread. This is the cup he will drink. This is the Father's will.

In the power of the Spirit, the Son will carry out this plan and offer himself as a spotless sacrifice to the Father (Heb. 9:14). He is resolved to obey, and his obedience will bear fruit.

The Resolution in Jesus' Obedience

The scenes following Gethsemane show Jesus' resolute intention to see this plan through to the end. First, Judas comes to betray the Lord, bringing with him a violent mob bearing sharp swords and cruel clubs (Mark 14:43–44).

Before Judas gives the fatal sign, Jesus speaks. "Whom do you seek?" he asks (John 18:4).

"Jesus of Nazareth," they answer.

"I am he," says Jesus (v. 5).

When they hear Jesus speak, the soldiers and officers fall backward (v. 6). Such is the power of the divine Son's word.

Jesus asks them again, "Whom do you seek?" (v. 7)

"Jesus of Nazareth," they say again.

"I told you that I am he. So, if you seek me, let these men go" (v. 8).

That's when Judas kisses Jesus (Mark 14:45). They seize him (v. 46), but the disciples are ready to fight back. Peter brandishes his sword and, in one deadly swipe, cuts off the ear of Malchus (v. 47; John 18:10). Jesus responds by telling him to put his sword away and asking, "Shall I not drink the cup that the Father has given me?" (John 18:11).

Then, Jesus calmly addresses the mob: "Have you come out as against a robber, with swords and clubs to capture me? Day after day I was with you in the temple teaching, and you did not seize me"

(Mark 14:48–49a). This is clearly overkill. Jesus will not resist arrest. "But," he says, "let the Scriptures be fulfilled" (v. 49b).

Now the disciples flee (v. 50), and Jesus is carried away to endure a long night of mockery and scorn. The series of unjust trials in kangaroo courts that follows is motivated by the malice of religious hypocrites, aided and abetted by the expedience of political cowards.

These details in the gospel accounts of that night reveal both the divine purpose and the voluntary nature of Jesus' obedience and death. From one perspective, it is right for us to say that Jesus was the victim of human injustice and cruelty: "He was oppressed, and he was afflicted, yet he opened not his mouth; like a lamb that is led to the slaughter, and like a sheep that before its shearers is silent, so he opened not his mouth" (Isa. 53:7). But he was not helpless: "I lay down my life that I may take it up again. No one takes it from me, but I lay it down of my own accord. I have authority to lay it down, and I have authority to take it up again" (John 10:17b–18a). Jesus died unjustly, but he was no mere victim; he died as a high priest solemnly offering himself as a sacrifice to God.[15]

As such, his obedient sacrifice bore fruit.

The Fruit of Jesus' Obedience

What was the fruit of the Son's obedience? Hebrews 5 gives us the answer:

> In the days of his flesh, Jesus offered up prayers and
> supplications, with loud cries and tears, to him who was able to
> save him from death, and he was heard because of his reverence.
> Although he was a son, he learned obedience through what
> he suffered. And being made perfect, he became the source of
> eternal salvation to all who obey him, being designated by God a
> high priest after the order of Melchizedek.
>
> Hebrews 5:7–10

Here we see Jesus—described in terms of his human nature, his divine sonship, and his high priesthood—learning obedience through suffering and achieving salvation for his people. As we've already observed, his true humanity is evident in the "loud cries and tears" that marked his prayers. The Father had affirmed his sonship at his baptism and transfiguration. But the writer has his priesthood especially in view here. For it was as a high priest that Jesus "offered up" prayers and then offered himself to God in the power of the eternal Spirit, without blemish, once and for all, as a sacrifice for sins, to effect the salvation and sanctification of his people (Heb. 7:27; 9:14, 28; 10:10–14).

Every phrase in that last sentence is important: Jesus was a high priest, charged with the responsibilities of both intercession (offering prayers) and sacrifice (offering himself). He discharged these duties in the power of the eternal Spirit—the same Spirit by whom he was miraculously conceived in the virgin's womb, and the same Spirit who descended upon him when he stood in the muddy waters of the Jordan. Indeed, "the Spirit was the constant companion of the Son,"[16] and he would now strengthen the Son in his greatest work.

But there's more. Jesus did not simply offer himself, but did so without blemish. His was the perfect sacrifice—the one spotless, acceptable offering. He also offered himself "once and for all," in a single satisfactory sacrifice, never to be repeated again. He offered himself to God, whose glory and honor was his great aim, whose will was his very meat and drink. And he offered himself as a sacrifice for sins, to effect both expiation (the removal of sins) and propitiation (the appeasing of wrath). His purpose through it all was to save and sanctify his people: to rescue them from wrath and to consecrate them, in and through his own holy sacrifice to God.

Nothing should move us to abhor our sins and adore our Savior's love more than these meditations on his sorrow in Gethsemane. Jesus' agony in the garden reveals both the horror that awaited him in the cup and the cross as well as the unfathomable love that kept him treading the lonely Via Dolorosa—the way of sorrows.

Christ's heartbreaking prayers in the shadow of Calvary should move us to mournfully sing with Elisabeth Clephane:

> And from my stricken heart with tears,
> Two wonders I confess;
> The wonder of redeeming love
> And my unworthiness.[17]

8

With Jesus in the Court: *Trial*

For our sake he made him to be sin who knew no sin, so that in
him we might become the righteousness of God.

2 Corinthians 5:21

In his essay, "God in the Dock," C. S. Lewis described how ancient
and modern people perceive God differently. "The ancient man," said
Lewis, "approached God (or even the gods) as the accused person
approaches his judge. For the modern man the roles are reversed. He
is the judge: God is in the dock."[1] This is true, as far as it goes. But
the reality is that God was "in the dock" long before the modernity in
which Lewis wrote his essay. For God allowed himself to be judged
by man when the God-man, Jesus Christ, was placed on trial in the
courts of Caiaphas, Pilate, and Herod.

In our rush to get from the garden to the cross and resurrection,
it is easy for us to pass too quickly over the trials of Jesus. Yet the
gospel writers take their time telling the story and include important
details designed not only to inform us about what happened, but also
to nourish and strengthen our faith. Let's also, then, take the time to
stand with Jesus in the court, witnessing the charges, the verdict, and
the sentence.

The Charges

Jesus was charged with two crimes: blasphemy and treason.

The charge of blasphemy is implicit in the final paragraph of Luke 22. Having sought the Father in the olive groves of Gethsemane, Jesus is ready to drink the cup of wrath and judgment in submission to his Father's will (v. 42). The temple guards arrive and seize him, taking him to the house of the high priest where Jesus is mocked, blindfolded, and blasphemed (vv. 63–65). Day breaks. And now the Sanhedrin questions Jesus about his identity:

Munus Triplex

Since the time of Calvin, Reformed theology has given regular attention to the *munus triplex*, or the three "offices" of Christ: prophet, priest, and king. "Christ" is a title that corresponds to the Hebrew word for "Messiah," meaning "anointed." Christ's offices meet our needs:

1. Prophet. Blinded by sin, we are engulfed in dark ignorance and thus need Christ as our prophet to speak God's Word, reveal the Father, and illuminate us by his Spirit.
2. Priest. In addition to ignorance, sin brings guilt, making us unfit for God's presence. But as our high priest, Jesus atones for sins through the offering of himself to God. Even more, he intercedes for us, pleading the merits of his own sacrifice on our behalf. As a merciful and faithful high priest, Jesus both sympathizes with our weaknesses and restores bold confidence to our relationship with God.
3. King. As our king, Jesus breaks the thralldom of our enemies—Satan, sin, death, and hell—defeating them by his cross and resurrection. We are thus transferred from the domain of darkness and made citizens of Christ's kingdom.

Jesus fulfilled these offices in his ministry by preaching the gospel, revealing the Father, thwarting the powers of darkness, offering his life as a perfect sacrifice, and interceding for his own. In his trial and crucifixion, Christ's three-fold office stands in sharp relief against the blasphemy of the priests, the injustice of Pilate and King Herod, and the scoffing of soldiers who dare him to prophesy and clothe him in mock regalia—a purple robe, a reed scepter, and a crown of thorns. Little did they know that through his death, Jesus would reveal the glory of God (as prophet), atone for our sins (as priest), and vanquish our mortal enemies (as king).[2]

"If you are the Christ, tell us." But he said to them, "If I tell you, you will not believe, and if I ask you, you will not answer. But from now on the Son of Man shall be seated at the right hand of the power of God." So they all said, "Are you the Son of God, then?" And he said to them, "You say that I am."

Luke 22: 67–70

Jesus, who had sweat drops of blood in his agonizing garden prayers (v. 44), now stands poised and serene. Without directly answering any of the council's questions, Jesus lays claim to three titles: Messiah, Son of Man, and Son of God. And this is enough to seal his fate, so far as the Jewish court is concerned. "What further testimony do we need? We have heard it ourselves from his own lips" (v. 71). What is implicit here Mark makes explicit: the high priest tears his clothes, claims Jesus blasphemed, and calls for a vote in which "they all condemned him as deserving death" (14:63–64).

What irony! The blasphemers charge the Son of God with blasphemy! The high priest of Israel condemns the true High Priest to an undeserved death!

But there is a problem. Though the council has found Jesus worthy of death, they have no authority to execute him (John 18:31), and the charge of blasphemy will be inconsequential in a Roman court. Jesus is therefore taken to Pilate and charged with treason: "We found this man misleading our nation and forbidding us to give tribute to Caesar, and saying that he himself is Christ, a king" (Luke 23:2). This, of course, was a half-truth. Jesus had admitted to being the Christ, but he wasn't guilty of insurrection. In fact, he had sanctioned the payment of Roman tribute (Luke 20:22–25). Pilate discerns as much, as he indicates with his verdict.

The Verdict

"Not guilty." This was the judgment of the Roman court (Luke 23:4). And this verdict is confirmed again and again in what Sinclair Ferguson calls "a litany of acquittals."[3] Pilate repeats his exoneration in verse 14, Herod (the reigning puppet-king over Judea) evidently confirms Pilate's verdict in verse 15, and Pilate repeats his acquittal a third time in verse 22: "Why, what evil has he done? I have found in him no guilt deserving death. I will therefore punish and release him." Later in the chapter, the sinless Son of God is crucified between two thieves. One rails while the other defends Jesus: "Do you not fear God, since you are under the same sentence of condemnation? And we indeed justly, for we are receiving the due reward of our deeds; but this man has done nothing wrong" (vv. 40–41). Even Jesus' executioner recognizes his innocence: "Now when the centurion saw what had taken place, he praised God, saying, 'Certainly this man was innocent!'" (v. 47). The historical record thus reveals that, "Jesus was not falsely judged 'Guilty!' on the basis of a misreading of the evidence. He was executed, even though the verdict passed on Him was 'Innocent!'"[4]

The obvious question, then, is why? A just execution follows a trial only when the capital charges stick. When a defendant is declared "not guilty," the charges are dismissed and the defendant is set free. But in this trial, Jesus has few accusers, and most voices say he has done nothing wrong. They include one man executed at his side (the dying thief) as well as the centurion who actually carried out the sentence. Before that, those in charge of the trial (Pilate and Herod) even declared Jesus innocent.

The verdict is Not Guilty, but the sentence is Death.

What are we to make of this?

The answer is two-fold, both historical and theological.

Historically, we must understand that the crucifixion of Jesus was the greatest miscarriage of justice—in fact, the worst act of *in*justice—in human history. As Martin tersely summarized, "the arrest was unprovoked: the accusation, false: the trial, a mockery: the evidence, perjury: the sentence, unrighteous and malicious: its execution, murder."[5]

We must acknowledge multiple culprits in this travesty of justice, all with different reasons for their participation. Judas appears to have been motivated by greed (Matt. 26:14–16; John 12:3–8; Acts 1:18). Pilate's choice was driven by political expediency and fear (John 19:10), whereas the chief priests were compelled by envy (Mark 15:10). Some might argue that the soldiers merely followed orders, but their cruel mockery of

Jesus made their malicious enjoyment of the violent proceedings transparent (Luke 22:63–65; 23:36–37).

Only a hardened heart could read these narratives without realizing that "the greed, envy and fear which prompted their behavior also prompt ours."[6] The story of Jesus' trial should compel our own self-examination. As Horatius Bonar, a nineteenth-century Scottish pastor and hymn writer, wrote:

> 'Twas I that shed that sacred Blood,
> I nailed him to the Tree,
> I crucified the Christ of God,
> I joined the mockery.[7]

Theologically, the verdict in Jesus' trial shows us something even more profound. Jesus was innocent of the two crimes with which he was charged—blasphemy and treason—but we are all guilty of both. Though Jesus claimed equality with God, it wasn't blasphemy for him to do so, because he was God manifest in the flesh. Though he was a king, his kingdom was not of this world (John 18:36), and nothing in his life or ministry displayed or incited rebellion against the governing authorities.

> **Question 38:** Why did he suffer "under Pontius Pilate" as judge?
>
> **Answer:** So that he, though innocent, might be condemned by an earthly judge, and so free us from the severe judgment of God that was to fall on us.
>
> —*The Heidelberg Catechism*

Yet every human being is guilty of both blasphemy and treason against God.[8] Thus, the doctrine of substitutionary atonement is embedded and enacted in the actual details of Jesus' trial. We were the guilty sinners, while Jesus was "holy, innocent, unstained, separate from sinners" (Heb. 7:26). He was declared innocent, yet sentenced to death, while we who stand before God's judgment bar as condemned criminals go free. His life was given in exchange for ours.

Calvin not only agrees with this understanding of Jesus' trials, but also argues that these circumstances were necessary to God's saving plan:

To take away our condemnation, it was not enough for him to suffer any kind of death: to make satisfaction for our redemption a form of death had to be chosen in which he might free us both by transferring our condemnation to himself and by taking our guilt upon himself. If he had been murdered by thieves or slain in an insurrection by a raging mob, in such a death there would have been no evidence of satisfaction. But when he was arraigned before the judgment seat as a criminal, accused and pressed by testimony, and condemned by the mouth of the judge to die—we know by these proofs that he took the role of a guilty man and evildoer.[9]

Both historically and theologically, the verdict Jesus receives is truly stunning. They reveal his majesty and his innocence, his sufficiency and his substitution.

The Sentence

Though Pilate clearly knew Jesus was innocent, he condemned him as guilty. The sentence: scourging and crucifixion. So begins this "liturgy of shame."[10] Matthew, Mark, and John mention the scourging in a single verse (Matt. 27:26; Mark 15:15; John 19:1), while Luke passes over it altogether. But the scourging was as necessary as the crucifixion itself, for Jesus himself had said, "See, we are going up to Jerusalem, and everything that is written about the Son of Man by the prophets will be accomplished. For he will be delivered over to the Gentiles and will be mocked and shamefully treated and spit upon. And after *flogging him*, they will kill him, and on the third day he will rise" (Luke 18:31–33). Perhaps Isaiah 53:5 was the specific prophecy Jesus had in mind: "Upon him was the *chastisement* that brought us peace, and with his *wounds* [*stripes*, KJV] we are healed."

The scourging alone was often enough to kill the victim. Some years ago, an article in the *Journal of the American Medical Association* provided a description of the brutal flogging from a medical perspective, describing the cruel process in excruciating detail. The victim of scourging would be stripped naked. The back, buttocks, and legs were flogged: forcefully struck again and again with the flagelleum, a short whip of leather thongs embedded with small bits of iron and bone to tear through muscle. This usually left the victim in shock.[11]

What inhumanity we witness in the brutality and barbarity of these vicious misdeeds! Yet Jesus' loss of dignity was the means to restoring ours. "*Ecce homo* indeed," write Ferguson and Thomas, "Behold the man, now dehumanized by man, that we who have been unmanned in sin might become truly human again."[12]

As awful as the scourging was, what awaited him would be even worse. "So Pilate, wishing to satisfy the crowd, released for them Barabbas, and having scourged Jesus, he delivered him to be crucified" (Mark 15:15). There Jesus went, silently and willingly, carrying his cross until strength failed, the righteous one treading the path of sinners to the hill of execution.

The next chapter is devoted to understanding Jesus' cruel death on that rugged cruciform tree. But do not move too quickly away from the courts of Caiaphas, Pilate, and Herod, where Jesus was judicially condemned to die. In these courts, we see Christ's trials. We hear the charges, the guilty verdict, and the sentence of death. Now what? By faith, we can and must look upon Christ's condemnation as the means of "our own deliverance from all condemnation."[13]

From a human standpoint, the trial of Jesus was a mockery of justice. But in the foreordained and "definite plan and foreknowledge of God" (Acts 2:23), Jesus took upon himself the stripes of justice that we deserved, so that we could receive the "not guilty" verdict that he deserved. He was escorted into the home of a cruel high priest and received no compassion or sympathy; we, in turn, now have a merciful and faithful high priest who gives us boldness to come to the throne of grace in our time of need. In the courtyards of the priests, Jesus was denied by one his best friends who said, "I know not the man"; we, in turn, now hear the Friend of Sinners saying, "I know you by name." On that fateful night, Jesus' accusers brought false charges and false witnesses, but God says to us, "Who shall bring any charge against God's elect? It is God who justifies. Who is to condemn? Christ Jesus is the one who died—more than that, who was raised—who is at the right hand of God, who indeed is interceding for us"

(Rom. 8:33–34). Jesus, the incarnate Lord of glory, stood trial in a human court to have his sonship disputed and denied—indeed, to be blasphemed by the unclean lips of sinful men. We, in turn, find our sonship eternally secured, and we exclaim, "Behold, what manner of love the Father hath bestowed upon us, that we should be called the sons of God" (1 John 3:1, KJV).[14] In short, because Christ was sentenced to die, you and I can be pardoned and live.

The trials of Jesus remind us that the true Judge of men is the Man who has been judged in our place. He is no a stranger to our suffering. Be emboldened, then, dear Christian. Draw near to him in repentant faith.

9

With Jesus on the Tree: *Crucifixion*

> I have been crucified with Christ. It is no longer I who live, but
> Christ who lives in me. And the life I now live in the flesh I
> live by faith in the Son of God, who loved me and gave himself
> for me.
>
> Galatians 2:20

The *graffito blasfemo* is the earliest known pictorial depiction of the crucifixion of Jesus. Inscribed on a wall near Palestine Hill in Rome, the *graffito blasfemo* pictures a donkey fastened to a cross, carved into plaster. To the left of the crucified donkey stands a man raising his left hand in a gesture of worship. A caption, written in Greek, says, "Alexamenos worships his god."

This carving was discovered in 1857, but it probably dates back to the third century. Its transparent insult to Christianity starkly reminds us that the idea of a crucified God was scandalous in the ancient world. A crucified deity was a contradiction in terms. For the first-century Jew, to be hanged on a cross was to be cursed by God (Deut. 21:23). For the Gentile, the cross was an obscenity: "The very word 'cross' should be far removed not only from the person of a Roman citizen, but from his thoughts, his eyes and his ears," wrote

Cicero.[1] No wonder Paul called the message of the cross a *skandalon*, a stumbling block (1 Cor. 1:23).

And yet, the message of the cross stands firmly in the center of the Christian faith. John Stott is right: "There is ... no Christianity without the cross. If the cross is not central to our religion, ours is not the religion of Jesus."[2] Thus, the best of our hymns, both ancient and modern, exult in the glories of the cross. The words of "O Sacred Head, Now Wounded," notable for its mournful melody, come from a twelfth-century Latin hymn translated into English in 1830. The simpler African American spiritual "Were You There" was first published in 1899, and Johnny Cash recorded it in 1963. These two songs represent two extremely different cultures: the piety of the medieval European church and that of oppressed slaves in the American South. But they share a common theme in the cross.

Both of these hymns take us to the cross itself. "O Sacred Head, Now Wounded" has us look at and speak to Jesus suffering on the cross. "Were You There" repeatedly asks, "Were you there when they crucified my Lord?" The fact is that we were. And we did not merely watch, but each of us was with him there. "I have been crucified with Christ," writes the apostle Paul (Gal. 2:20). And again, "We know that our old self was crucified with him in order that the body of sin might be brought to nothing, so that we would no longer be enslaved to sin" (Rom. 6:6). This is true of every Christian. To be *in* Christ means he was crucified *for* us and we were crucified *with* him. When Jesus was suspended between heaven and earth on that rough-hewn tree atop Golgotha's lonely hill, his body broken and bruised, he hung there for me. And in some mysterious way, I hung there with him.

In this chapter we will study the account of Jesus' crucifixion given in Mark 15. There, Mark shows us how Jesus took our place, faced the darkness, and tore the veil. In theological language, these events teach us the doctrines of substitution, propitiation, and reconciliation.

On the Cross, Jesus Took Our Place: *Substitution*

When we see how Jesus took our place on the cross, we see again the doctrine of *substitution*, a running theme in our study. Substitutionary atonement is not an esoteric theological topic but a truth germane to the gospel. In fact, Paul starts here when he reminds the Corinthians of the essential message of the gospel: "For I delivered to you as of first importance what I also received: that *Christ died for our sins* in accordance with the Scriptures" (1 Cor. 15:3). Peter writes similarly, *"He himself bore our sins in his body on the tree*, that we might die to sin and live to righteousness. By his wounds you have been healed" (1 Peter 2:24).

O Sweet Exchange!

The doctrine of substitutionary atonement has inspired the joyful celebration of believers throughout the centuries. The anonymous second-century *Epistle to Diognetus* contains a moving confession of an early believer's hope in the "sweet exchange" of our sin for Christ's righteousness:

"When our iniquity had come to its full height, and it was clear beyond all mistaking that retribution in the form of punishment and death must be looked for, the hour arrived in which God had determined to make known from then onwards His loving-kindness and His power. How surpassing is the love and tenderness of God! In that hour, instead of hating us and rejecting us and remembering our wickednesses against us, He showed how long-suffering He is. He bore with us, and in pity He took our sins upon Himself and gave His Son as a ransom for us—the Holy for the wicked, the Sinless for sinners, the Just for the unjust, the Incorrupt for the corrupt, the Immortal for the mortal. For was there, indeed, anything except His righteousness that could have availed to cover our sins? In whom could we, in our lawlessness and ungodliness, have been made holy, but in the Son of God alone? O sweet exchange! O unsearchable working! O benefits unhoped for!—that the wickedness of multitudes should thus be hidden in the One holy, and the holiness of One should sanctify the countless wicked!"[3]

But Peter and Paul didn't invent the doctrine of substitution. They proclaimed it because they knew from firsthand experience that Jesus had given his life to ransom theirs. Christ had borne the judgment they deserved. This kindled their hearts, captured their imaginations, and compelled them to live with the singular ambition of making Christ known. "For the love of Christ controls us," writes Paul, "because we have concluded this: that one has died for all, therefore all have died; and he died for all, that those who live might no longer live for themselves but for him who for their sake died and was raised" (2 Cor. 5:14–15).

While the apostles *explained* the vicarious nature of the cross, the gospel records *illustrate* substitution by including the remarkable story of Barabbas, the condemned criminal whose freedom was secured by the ransom of Jesus' life. Barabbas was a first-class felon or, as Matthew writes, "a notorious prisoner" (Matt. 27:16). He was probably both a common thief (John 18:40) and an insurrectionist murderer (Mark 15:7).

Whereas Barabbas was guilty and deserved death, Jesus was innocent, vindicated by Pilate himself (Mark 15:14). But in the grossest miscarriage of justice in history, guilt-ridden Barabbas was released and walked away with undeserved freedom while the sinless Son of God was condemned, scourged, and crucified.

This story beckons us to self-identify with Barabbas, for Jesus is *our* substitute.[4] Like Barabbas, we have sinned and deserve judgment, but Jesus took our place, carried our sins, and bore our punishment while we go free. "For Christ also suffered once for sins, the righteous for the unrighteous, that he might bring us to God, being put to death in the flesh but made alive in the spirit" (1 Peter 3:18).

This is the core of the Christian faith—the living, beating, pulsing heart of the gospel itself. It should be no wonder, then, that painters and writers have often depicted this marvelous truth. Take, for example, a painting by one of my favorite artists, the seventeenth-century Dutch painter Rembrandt Harmenszoon van Rijn. In *Raising the Cross,* a painting of the crucifixion, Rembrandt painted himself in the scene as one of the Roman soldiers. It seems that he understood that his sins were responsible for Jesus' death. As the hymnist Philip Bliss wrote,

> Bearing shame and scoffing rude,
> In my place condemned He stood;
> Sealed my pardon with His blood.
> Hallelujah! What a Savior![5]

On the Cross, Jesus Faced the Darkness: *Propitiation*

Substitution is central to our understanding of the cross, but the Scriptures tell us more. For they not only explain that Jesus took our place on the cross, they also describe what he faced there. We, then, must think about the mysterious darkness that descended over the whole land, followed by Jesus' cry of dereliction and death.

The Darkness

Most people perceive darkness as ominous and threatening. Children, and sometimes adults, are afraid of the dark. And our intuitive responses to darkness fit the biblical perspective as well, for darkness in Scripture often symbolizes judgment. Jesus, for example, spoke of judgment in terms of

Question 30: Is it significant that he was "crucified" instead of dying some other way?

Answer: Yes. By this I am convinced that he shouldered the curse which lay on me, since death by crucifixion was cursed by God.

Question 40: Why did Christ have to suffer death?

Answer: Because God's justice and truth require it: nothing else could pay for our sins except the death of the Son of God.

—*The Heidelberg Catechism*

being cast into "outer darkness" where there will be "weeping and gnashing of teeth" (Matt 8:12; 22:13; 25:30).

Consider also the Old Testament. The next to last plague in Egypt, just prior to the death of the firstborn, was three days of "a darkness to be felt ... pitch darkness in all the land of Egypt" (Ex. 10:21–22). When the prophets uttered their oracles of doom over Israel and the nations and foretold God's judgment, they often described it in terms of darkness. Amos, for example, rebuked those who longed for the day of the Lord because they thought it would go well for them when instead it would be "darkness, and not light, and gloom with no brightness in it" (Amos 5:20).

Thus, when Mark tells us that the land was engulfed in darkness for three hours as Jesus hung on the cross (Mark 15:33), he tells us that God's judgment was falling on Jesus. This is substitution, but it is also *propitiation,* the appeasement of God's wrath against our sins.

For Jesus not only took our place, but he also bore the wrath and judgment we deserved.[6]

The hymn writer, Isaac Watts captures these truths in "Alas! and Did My Savior Bleed?"

> Was it for crimes that I had done
> He groaned upon the tree?
> Amazing pity! grace unknown!
> And love beyond degree!
>
> Well might the sun in darkness hide
> And shut His glory in,
> When Christ the mighty Maker died
> For man the creature's sin.[7]

The Cry

Following the darkness came Jesus' cry of dereliction in Mark 15:34, "'Eloi, Eloi, lema sabachthani?' which means, 'My God, my God, why have you forsaken me?'" These words come from Psalm 22, a song of lament that Jesus appropriately quoted in his hour of abandonment. But his cry lamented more than his pain, and even more than his death, for he lamented being forsaken by his Father. "Rabbi" Duncan said, "It was damnation, and he took it lovingly."[8]

Does this seem like too much? Is such language justifiable? Does a claim that Jesus was damned for our sins go beyond what Scripture actually says?

I grant that the Bible never uses that phrase. But it comes close. In Galatians 3:13, Paul says, "Christ redeemed us from the curse of the law *by becoming a curse for us*—for it is written, 'Cursed is everyone who is hanged on a tree.'" This is damnation—being cursed by God. We were under the curse (Gal. 3:10), and therefore deserved damnation. How then could we be saved? Only by a propitiatory sacrifice. Not just any substitute but a sin-bearing, wrath-absorbing, judgment-removing, curse-canceling substitute.

Cross Words

Every field of study has its own nomenclature, its specialized language. In biology, plants and animals are known by genus and species. Musicians use a specialized vocabulary that includes terms like pitch, rhythm, harmony, and form. Golfers have their own language too: backswing, birdie, bogie, eagle, par, hook, slice, and so on. And Christian theology has its own vocabulary, with some of the richest terms pertaining to the cross. Here are a few "cross words":

- **Atonement** and **expiation** refer to the covering of sin. Key texts: Leviticus 16 which describes Israel's annual Day of Atonement (Yom Kippur) and Hebrews 10 which describes Christ's singular sacrifice of himself.
- **Justification** is the judicial verdict God pronounces on sinners by virtue of Christ's obedience, righteousness, and death in their place. Key texts: Romans 3:21–26; 4–5.
- **Propitiation** is the appeasement of God's righteous wrath against sin. Key texts: Romans 3:25; 1 John 2:2; 4:10.
- **Ransom** refers to a payment made to secure the release of prisoners. Christ gave himself as a ransom for us. Key texts: Matthew 20:28; Mark 10:45; 1 Timothy 2:6; 1 Peter 1:18; Revelation 5:9.
- **Reconciliation** is a relational term describing the restored friendship between parties who had been separated by enmity and hostility. Key texts: 2 Corinthians 5:18–21; Ephesians 2:11–22 where both Gentiles and Jews are reconciled to God through the blood of the cross; and Colossians 1:19–23, which also describes the cosmic scope of reconciliation.
- **Redemption** is the freedom from slavery obtained through the payment of the ransom price. Key texts: Exodus 6:6 (and indeed the whole exodus story, where God redeems Israel from slavery in Egypt); Romans 3:24; Ephesians 1:7; Colossians 1:14.
- **Sanctification** isn't just a word for our moral transformation, but also a term that means to be set apart for God. On the cross, Jesus sanctified himself and in so doing sanctified us. Key texts: John 17:19; 1 Corinthians 1:30; Hebrews 2:11; 10:10, 14.
- **Triumph** describes Christ's glorious victory over evil through the cross. Key texts: Genesis 3:15 where God promises that the woman's seed will crush the serpent; Mighty Warrior passages such as Exodus 15 and Zephaniah 3:17; John 12:31; Colossians 2:15; and the book of Revelation.[9]

This truth captures at once the terror of our sin and the glory of our God. John Stott wrote, "God could quite justly have abandoned us to our fate. He could have left us alone to reap the fruit of our wrongdoing and to perish in our sins. It is what we deserved. But he did not do that. Because he loved us, he came after us in Christ. He pursued us even to the desolate anguish of the cross, where he bore our sin, guilt, judgment and death."[10] As the cross reveals the severity of our sin, so it also reveals the ability and desire of Christ to bear the punishment for our sin.

Many people, of course, raise moral objections to the whole concept of Christ's propitiatory and substitutionary sacrifice. But rejecting Christ's curse-bearing death leaves us with an even bigger problem. We are left asking how a good God could allow the righteous to suffer. Almost no one thinks Jesus was evil. Even many skeptics who reject his divinity will agree that Jesus was good. Yet he suffered, and suffered horribly. Here is the best of men who dies the worst of deaths. It forces us to ask if there is any justice in the world at all. If Jesus died for no purpose, then the whole moral fabric of the universe begins to unravel.

F. W. Krummacher, in his classic study *The Suffering Savior*, addresses this question. After describing the scourging and mockery of Jesus, he asks, "How can we reconcile such revolting occurrences with the government of a just and holy God! A great mystery must lie at the bottom of them, or our belief in a supreme moral government loses its support." Krummacher then answers, "What befalls Christ befalls us in him, who is our representative.... Our hell is extinguished in Jesus' wounds; our curse is consumed in Jesus' soul; our guilt is purged away in Jesus' blood."[11] Neither the clear testimony of Scripture nor sane moral judgment will allow us to say that Jesus suffered for his own sins. No, he died there *for us*—in *our* place, bearing *our* sins, enduring *our* judgment, forsaken by the Father. Indeed, "He himself bore our sins in his body on the tree" (1 Peter 2:24a).

On the Cross, Jesus Tore the Curtain: *Reconciliation*

Jesus took our place, facing the darkness of God's judgment and wrath against our sins. Then, "Jesus uttered a loud cry and breathed his last. And the curtain of the temple was torn in two, from top to bottom" (Mark 15:37–38).

The Jerusalem temple had two veils—one that separated the rest of the temple from the Holy of Holies, the place where God's presence dwelled, and another that separated the Court of Israel from the Court of Women and the Court of the Gentiles. There are good theological reasons for thinking either veil was the one torn. The curtain at the Holy of Holies makes sense given its symbolism (cf. Heb. 6:19; 10:20) as a special place entered by only one man, the high priest, and on only one day each year, on the Day of Atonement. But the second veil, which was more visible to the public, also makes sense as in Christ there is no Jew or Gentile, male or female (Gal. 3:28). Whichever curtain, Scripture indicates that it was torn to demonstrate two things: (1) God was finished with the temple and the old covenant system of worship, and (2) the way into God's holy presence was now open. In short, Jesus had removed the barrier.

> Therefore, brothers, since we have confidence to enter the holy places by the blood of Jesus, by the new and living way that he opened for us through the curtain, that is, through his flesh, and since we have a great priest over the house of God, let us draw near with a true heart in full assurance of faith, with our hearts sprinkled clean from an evil conscience and our bodies washed with pure water.
>
> Hebrews 10:19–22

The one word that sums up this passage is *reconciliation*. Through substitution, Jesus took our place. In taking our place, he faced the darkness of God's wrath and judgment. That's propitiation. But the result of propitiation is the torn curtain. It is reconciliation. We are reconciled to God and given access into his presence.

Notice how skillfully Mark illustrates the profound, world-altering significance of the torn veil by describing what happens afterward. First, the Roman centurion who had overseen Jesus' execution makes a remarkable confession: "Truly this man was the Son of God!" (15:39). In Mark's narrative, the centurion is the first person to recognize Jesus' divine sonship. He's not an insider, but an outsider. Not a Jew, but a Gentile. Not a disciple, but a centurion. Not a friend, but an enemy. And now he makes a confession of faith!

Then, Mark 15:40–41 mentions a group of women who watched from a distance. I'll say more about this in the next chapter, but the presence of the women in Mark's narrative argues for both the authenticity of Mark's record as well as the reconciling power of the cross. For here the women (who were forbidden to enter the inner court of the temple) make up the inner circle of Jesus' disciples and will be the first eyewitnesses to his burial and resurrection (15:47–16:1).

Finally, in verses 42–46, Mark highlights the role of Joseph of Arimathea in Jesus' burial. Joseph was a Pharisee and a member of the Sanhedrin, the ruling council partially responsible for Jesus' arrest and trial. The Pharisees instigated the crucifixion, but one of their own openly cared for Jesus' body.

Mark's details thus show us how the cross brings reconciliation, not only in the vertical dimension between man and God, but also on the horizontal level between all different kinds of people. It foreshadows the birth of the Christian church, a new society of people made up of both Jews and Gentiles, both men and women, both Jesus' disciples and his former enemies, all reconciled to God as part of a single new humanity (cf. Gal. 3:28; Eph. 2:11–22; Col. 3:11).

Remember how Rembrandt included himself among the soldiers in his painting *The Raising of the Cross*? You may also know that he painted himself in *Descent from the Cross*, placing himself among those who cared for Jesus' body after death. Perhaps Rembrandt understood that he was responsible for Jesus' death *and* that he was reconciled by his death. So it is with all who believe.

The cross represents not only what happened to Jesus of Nazareth in first-century Jerusalem, but also what has happened to every person united to him through faith. If you believe in Jesus, then his death counts as yours. He was *your* substitute and representative. He took *your* place. He is *your* great high priest. He bore *your* name on his heart as he "through the eternal Spirit offered himself without blemish to God" (Heb. 9:14). *Your* sins were judged when the darkness descended on Jesus. *Your* record was cleared. What Jesus did, he did for *you*. Christ's work is made *yours*. Like Paul, we can say, "I have been crucified with Christ. It is no longer I who live, but Christ who lives in me. And the life I now live in the flesh I live by faith in the Son of God, who loved me and gave himself for me" (Gal. 2:20).

"Were you there when they crucified the Lord?"

Yes. Yes, you were.

10

With Jesus in His Life: *Resurrection*

We were buried therefore with him by baptism into death, in order that, just as Christ was raised from the dead by the glory of the Father, we too might walk in newness of life. For if we have been united with him in a death like his, we shall certainly be united with him in a resurrection like his.

Romans 6:4–5

The resurrection of Jesus, alongside the incarnation and crucifixion, is one of the central historical events in the Christian faith. Without the resurrection there would be no Christianity. "If Christ has not been raised," wrote the apostle Paul, "then our preaching is in vain and your faith is in vain" (1 Cor. 15:14). For this reason, John Updike, a Pulitzer Prize-winning American author, began his poem "Seven Stanzas at Easter" by proclaiming the significance of the physical resurrection:

> Make no mistake: if He rose at all
> it was as His body;
> if the cells' dissolution did not reverse, the molecules reknit,
>   the amino acids rekindle,
> the Church will fall.[1]

I am a Christian because I believe in the resurrection. I am convinced that after dying a violent death on a Roman cross on a Friday afternoon in AD 30, Jesus of Nazareth came back to life and emerged from the tomb on Sunday morning. This is not easy to believe. But if true, it is not merely central to Christianity but the most pivotal event in human history.

This chapter will follow the story of Christ's resurrection recorded in the gospel of Matthew. We will consider the nature of the resurrection, the evidence for the resurrection, and the ongoing significance of the resurrection for us today.

The Nature of the Resurrection

Christianity teaches that Jesus of Nazareth, who had been crucified under Pontius Pilate and was buried, rose from the dead on the third day and came *physically* back to life. As Herman Bavinck writes, "The resurrection was the event in which Christ by his divine power revived his dead body, united it with his soul, and thus left the tomb."[2] We see this clearly in Matthew's gospel. First, an angel announces Jesus' resurrection to Mary Magdalene and the other Mary, mother of James and John, who have come to visit his tomb:

> "Do not be afraid, for I know that you seek Jesus who was crucified. He is not here, for he has risen, as he said. Come, see the place where he lay. Then go quickly and tell his disciples that he has risen from the dead, and behold, he is going before you to Galilee; there you will see him. See, I have told you."
>
> Matthew 28:5–7

Matthew then records two appearances Jesus made. As we will see, these stories help establish the authenticity of Matthew's record. But let's not skip ahead to what the appearances accomplish forensically. Let's first focus on the sensory details of the appearances themselves.

Notice that they *saw* him: the women in verse 9 and the disciples in verse 17. They also *heard* him: Jesus spoke to the disciples, saying "Greetings!" (v. 9), and Jesus gave them the Great Commission in verses 18–20. Finally, they *touched* him. The women "came up and *took hold of his feet* and worshiped him" (v. 9b). But the most famous tactile encounter with the risen Jesus comes later when "doubting Thomas" meets Jesus in the upper room:

> Now Thomas, one of the twelve, called the Twin, was not with them when Jesus came. So the other disciples told him, "We have seen the Lord." But he said to them, "Unless I see in his hands the mark of the nails, and place my finger into the mark of the nails, and place my hand into his side, I will never believe." Eight days later, his disciples were inside again, and Thomas was with them. Although the doors were locked, Jesus came and stood among them and said, "Peace be with you." Then he said to Thomas, "Put your finger here, and see my hands; and put out your hand, and place it in my side. Do not disbelieve, but believe." Thomas answered him, "My Lord and my God!" Jesus said to him, "Have you believed because you have seen me? Blessed are those who have not seen and yet have believed."
>
> John 20:24–29

These sensory details show us that the resurrection of Jesus was *physical*. The resurrection cannot be explained as the disciples' vague consciousness that Jesus somehow remained with them even after death. Nor do the stories represent the disciples' comfort that Jesus had gone on to heaven, assuring them of an afterlife. No, *the resurrection was a physical, material, embodied reality*. The very same body that was scourged, crucified, wrapped in linens, and laid in the tomb had now returned to life.

If the resurrection was not the physical, bodily return of Jesus from the grave, then the gospel records are false. But we know that the apostles did not imagine this or describe it as something other than it was. Instead, they simply testified to what they had seen and heard and touched (see 1 John 1:1–3a). Any attempt to demystify the resurrection and turn it into something less physical is not only a denial of the historical record and a compromise of Scripture, but is averse to the gospel itself.

The Evidence for the Resurrection

Whole books have, of course, been written in defense of the historicity of Jesus' resurrection. For readers who have doubts, I recommend N. T. Wright's massive study *The Resurrection of the Son of God.*[3] Its 800 pages deserve careful investigation. But we will look at three lines of evidence that emerge from Matthew's record: the women as eyewitnesses, the cover-up plot, and the worshiping missionaries.

The Eyewitnesses

Interestingly, the first witnesses that Matthew cites as seeing the risen Lord were women (Matt. 28:1–10). Few initial readers would have found this persuasive since the eyewitness testimony of women was not accepted in either Roman or Jewish jurisprudence. In fact, in the earliest known written critique of Christianity (called "The True Word" and written in AD 175), the author attempted to discredit the resurrection as mere story precisely because it had been told first by women.[4]

But the fact that women were the first eyewitnesses is actually strong evidence for the authenticity of the resurrection. The whole account ironically makes the leaders of the church (the apostles) look bad and reveals the women as the heroes of the story. Whatever the resurrection stories are, then, they are clearly *not* fabricated by the early church. If they had been made up, they would have gone very differently. The only conceivable reason the early Christians had for writing the reports as they did is that those reports are true.

The Cover-Up

Similarly telling is the cover-up plot hatched by the chief priests and elders in collusion with the soldiers guarding the tomb (Matt. 28:11–15). On one level, the cover-up serves as a smoking gun since everybody knows that a cover-up means there must be a story. That is, the tomb must have been empty. As Wright noted, "This sort of story could only have any point at all in a community where the empty tomb was an absolute and unquestioned datum."[5] So the plot to conceal the resurrection indicates that it really happened. If the body had not gone missing and the tomb remained occupied, there would have been no need to pay off soldiers and invent the stolen body story. Further, Matthew's report of this story indicates his full confidence in the bodily resurrection of Jesus. If the "stolen body" accusation had not risen, Matthew wouldn't have invented it. Why should he? On the other hand, if Matthew himself had any lingering doubt concerning Jesus' resurrection, he wouldn't have included the cover-up plot in his narrative. The fact that Matthew did include the story shows just how deeply persuaded he was that Jesus did, in fact, rise from the dead.

The cover-up itself reveals how the report of Jesus' resurrection threatened the religious leaders. They didn't want this to be true. Neither did they want others to believe it had happened. Why? Because Jesus' resurrection vindicated his claims: if Jesus is raised from the dead, he is indeed the Messiah, the Christ, the Son of God.

A few years ago, I read an article entitled "Save Jesus, Ignore Easter" in which Erik Reese basically argued that Christians pay too much attention to the resurrection and should spend more time following Jesus' teachings.[6] The problem with this approach is that it means picking and choosing what we want out of Jesus' words. If Jesus really did rise from the dead, then he really was who he said he was. And that means we *can't* approach his teachings as mere moral advice apart from who he is as Savior, nor can we choose among the teachings cafeteria-style. If Jesus really did rise from the dead, then he really is the Son of God, and we must embrace him *and* everything he teaches.

The Worshiping Missionaries

The final paragraph of Matthew's gospel presents a third line of evidence for the resurrection: the disciples worshiped him (Matt. 28:16–20). Notice that even though Jesus appeared to them, some doubted (v. 17). This shows just how unexpected the resurrection was to them. Even those closest to Jesus were not looking for it. It couldn't have been the product of the grieved disciples' wishful thinking. They too needed convincing. But some worshiped him (v. 17). And they heeded his command—what we now know as the Great Commission (v. 19–20)—to take his gospel to all nations and baptize others in the name of the Father, Son, and Holy Spirit. First-century Jews did not worship crucified men or angels or ghosts. Nor did they go around baptizing and forming new communities with Gentiles, centered on following the teachings of potential Messiahs who had been killed. Something happened that convinced them that Jesus of Nazareth had risen from the dead, thus vindicating his claim to be the Son of God.

This is a large part of Wright's case for the historicity of Jesus' resurrection. What else could account for how this Jesus-movement started out of Judaism? There has never been anything like it before or since. Again, the most rational explanation is that these disciples truly did see alive the same Jesus whom they had seen crucified.[7] These monotheistic Jewish fishermen, who came to worship Jesus as the Christ and herald the good news of his kingdom as the first missionaries, really were eyewitnesses of his resurrection.

The Significance of the Resurrection

We have now considered the historical evidence for the resurrection, but why does it matter? What significance does the resurrection have for you and me today? In brief, the resurrection gives us hope. It affirms God's forgiveness and announces the defeat of death. It also reveals how God's grace renews and restores the created order. Thus, the resurrection assures us that Christ is with us and we with him.

The Resurrection Assures Us of God's Forgiveness

Try to imagine being Mary Magdalene before she witnessed Jesus' resurrection (Matt. 28:1). Luke tells us that she had once been in the grip of evil and Jesus delivered her, casting out seven demons (Luke 8:2). Who knows what the horrors of her life had been? Often identified as a prostitute forgiven by Jesus, though the New Testament never identifies her as such, she was certainly an outcast whose life Jesus had changed. Now she believed that Jesus was dead. She had seen his crucifixion and had now come to the tomb, Mark tells us, to anoint his body in burial (Mark 16:1). She clearly didn't expect Jesus to rise from the dead. No one did. We can only imagine what she must have thought. Here was the man who had liberated her, forgiven her sins, given her dignity, transformed her life. Now he had died a criminal's death.

Maybe she wondered if all Jesus had seemed to do for her was now undone. Maybe his forgiveness and her freedom were now called into question. Would the dark demons of her past return? Would she once again be treated as a social outcast? Was there any hope? Then she sees the empty tomb. She hears the angel's announcement: "He is not here, for he has risen" (Matt. 28:6). She departs from the tomb trembling with joyful fear (v. 8). And then, in verse 9, she actually sees him, hears him! So she falls down, touches his feet, and worships him. He is alive, and that means she really is free. What assurance this must have given her!

In John Bunyan's famous allegory, *The Pilgrim's Progress*, a man on a journey carries a large and heavy burden on his back. The burden represents the weight of his past: his sin and guilt. The one thing he wants is to have that burden loosed, but no one he sees, nor anything he tries, can remove it ... until he comes to the cross. Then, the burden rolls off his back. But it does not roll just anywhere: significantly, it rolls down the hill into an open tomb. And the man sings out because he knows the man who died on that cross but then walked out of that grave took all his shame away.[8]

The resurrection assures us of God's forgiveness. It shows us that the burden of our past, including all our sin and guilt, has rolled off our shoulders and onto the scourged and bleeding back of Jesus so to be buried forever in his empty tomb! That's why Paul says, "If Christ has not been raised, your faith is futile and you are still in your sins" (1 Cor. 15:17). But he *has* been raised. He "was delivered up for our trespasses and raised for our justification" (Rom. 4:25). Now we are free. The resurrection proclaims the complete sufficiency of his redemptive work for us. It is "the 'Amen!' of the Father upon the 'It is finished!' of the Son."[9] His resurrection declares our vindication. In the words of John Wilbur Chapman,

Living, He loved me; dying, He saved me;
Buried, He carried my sins far away;

Rising, He justified freely forever:
One day He's coming—O glorious day![10]

The Resurrection Declares that Death Is Defeated Once and for All

In his resurrection, Jesus defeated death itself. As Peter proclaimed on the day of Pentecost, "God raised him up, loosing the pangs of death, because it was not possible for him to be held by it" (Acts 2:24). Or as Paul says in Romans 6:9, "We know that Christ, being raised from the dead, will never die again; death no longer has dominion over him." In Revelation 1:17–18, the risen Christ himself says

> **Question 45:** How does Christ's resurrection benefit us?
>
> **Answer:** First, by his resurrection he has overcome death, so that he might make us share in the righteousness he obtained for us by his death. Second, by his power we too are already raised to a new life. Third, Christ's resurrection is a sure pledge to us of our blessed resurrection.
>
> —*The Heidelberg Catechism*

"Fear not, I am the first and the last, and the living one. I died, and behold I am alive forevermore, and I have the keys of Death and Hades." Simply put, death lost its grip on Jesus.

Jesus defeated death not only for himself, but also for us. He died and rose as a new representative for humanity, as the second Adam. "But in fact Christ has been raised from the dead," writes Paul, "the firstfruits of those who have fallen asleep. For as by a man came death, by a man has come also the resurrection of the dead. For as in Adam all die, so also in Christ shall all be made alive" (1 Cor. 15:20–22). This fact that we will be made truly alive, new, and whole, is central to the good news. The empty tomb assures us that sickness and suffering, death and disease will not have the final word. "The King of glory has conquered the king of terrors."[11]

The resurrection gives me great hope, and for personal reasons. I mentioned earlier that I have terrible eyesight because of a degenerative eye disorder called keratoconus. One of my children has Type 1 diabetes, is insulin dependent, and receives several injections a day. My precious mother, only halfway into her 60s, has advanced Alzheimer's and has not recognized me for several years. But the resurrection of Jesus means the day is coming when Mom will know me again, and my son will never need another shot, and I will see with 20/20 vision. These are but three future realities dear to me when more than this, our God will wipe every tear away, and all death will die, and no one will mourn or cry or feel pain ever again (Rev. 21:4).

Indeed, "all of this is a consequence of the resurrection of Jesus."[12] The resurrection guarantees that death and dying will be no more. The resurrection shouts for all to hear, "Death be not proud! Death has lost its victory! Death has lost its sting! Yes, death itself has worked backwards! Our great enemy has been defeated once and for all!"[13]

The Resurrection Reveals How God's Grace Brings Renewal and Restoration to the Created Order

The resurrection not only proves the death of death. It also shows us how God's grace brings renewal and restoration to the entire created order. In his 1947 book *Miracles*, C. S. Lewis wrote that Christ's resurrection "forced open a door that has been locked since the death of the first man. He has met, fought, and beaten the King of Death" and therefore, "a new chapter in cosmic history has opened."[14] The resurrection declares that grace restores nature, thus affirming the basic goodness of the material world and underscoring the comprehensive scope of renewal ushered in by the new creation.[15]

When Jesus emerged from the tomb in a physical body, it was God's definitive stamp of approval on the creation project in all its materiality. This is why the early Christians both looked to the future with confidence that the created order itself would be redeemed and threw their lives into serving others inside and outside their own communities in the present brokenness of the world. They knew that the creation was groaning, waiting for full redemption (see Rom. 8:19–23).

The resurrection of Christ therefore has implications for both our present and our future. The physical body of Christ, raised from the tomb in glory, is a signpost for the age to come. The king of death has been defeated. The Lord of life reigns. And he will extend the healing power of his reign over every square inch of this planet. This is the future glory for which we wait.

Grateful, Glorified Knees

When Joni Eareckson Tada was only seventeen years old, she was injured in a diving accident and paralyzed from the neck down. Joni continued to practice her Christian faith, but being a quadriplegic brought obvious limitations to her life, including her worship. In one of her books, she recalls attending a convention where the speaker closed the service by asking everyone to kneel for prayer. There she sat in her wheelchair as five or six hundred people went to their knees, while she could not. "I couldn't stop the tears," she writes. But her tears weren't tears of self-pity.

"Tears were streaming because I was struck with the beauty of seeing so many people on bended knees before the Lord. It was a picture of heaven.

Sitting there, I was reminded that in heaven I will be free to jump up, dance, kick, and do aerobics. Although I'm sure Jesus will be delighted to watch me rise on tiptoe, there's something I plan to do that may please Him more. If possible, somewhere, sometime before the party gets going, sometime before the guests are called to the banquet table at the Wedding Feast of the Lamb, the first thing I plan to do on resurrected legs is to drop on grateful, glorified knees. I will quietly kneel at the feet of Jesus....

I with shriveled, bent fingers, atrophied muscles, gnarled knees, and no feeling from the shoulders down, will one day have a new body, light, bright, and clothed in righteousness—powerful and dazzling....

No other religion, no other philosophy promises new bodies, hearts and minds. Only in the Gospel of Christ do hurting people find such incredible hope."[16]

But the dawn of this new day is already upon us. As people of the resurrection, we are therefore tasked with the present work of extending God's reign into every possible nook and cranny of the present world. That's why we not only proclaim the gospel of the crucified and risen Christ, but also feed orphans, build hospitals, adopt children, clothe the naked, serve the homeless, fight human trafficking, revitalize our neighborhoods, and wisely steward our natural resources, all in Jesus' name. The resurrection shows us that matter matters.

The Resurrection Assures us that Christ Is with Us and We with Him

We have seen the significance of the resurrection in assuring us that God has forgiven sinners, delivering us from death and renewing the creation. But in each of these, we see once more the running theme in this book: our union with Christ. He is with us and we are with him through the Spirit in power. The resurrection shows us just how Christ is with us here now and we are with him as well.

At the end of Matthew 28, Jesus gives his disciples what we call the Great Commission and then says, "Behold, I am with you always, to the end of the age" (v. 20). We know that Jesus will not actually go with each of the disciples as they carry out the Great Commission. In fact, he will soon ascend to the Father and not remain on earth at all. So what does Jesus mean here? How will he never leave the disciples? We get a clue from how Luke and John finish their gospels. In Luke 24:49, Jesus says, "Behold, I am sending the promise of my Father upon you. But stay in the city until you are clothed with power from on high." And in John 20:21–22, he says, "Peace be with you. As the Father has sent me, even so I am sending you.... Receive the Holy Spirit."

Jesus is with us through the gift of his Spirit who dwells in us and with us. By pouring his Spirit on the church at Pentecost, and through the Spirit's abiding presence in the hearts and lives of believers, the risen and exalted Christ continues to work in and through his church as he extends his kingdom in the world.

So the resurrection means that Christ abides with us through the Spirit, but it also means that we live with him now. We enjoy present union with him in his resurrection. As Paul repeats again and again in his letters, we were raised with Christ (e.g. Eph. 1:19–20; 2:4–6; Col. 2:12; 3:1). Jesus' resurrection was his vindication, through which he was "declared to be the Son of God in power" (Rom. 1:4), but it was also the vindication of all who believe. As Paul says in Romans 4:25, Jesus was "delivered up for our trespasses and *raised for our justification."*

The resurrection changed everything! When Jesus rose from the dead, he defeated death, leaving its sinister power behind him in the tomb. And he unlocked the gates of eternal life so that the power of the future age came flooding into the present world.[17] The resurrection therefore affects how we live in the here and now.

> Do you not know that all of us who have been baptized into Christ Jesus were baptized into his death? We were buried therefore with him by baptism into death, in order that, just as Christ was raised from the dead by the glory of the Father, we too might walk in newness of life.
>
> For if we have been united with him in a death like his, we shall certainly be united with him in a resurrection like his.
>
> Romans 6:3–5

When Jesus died on the cross to destroy the power of sin, you and I died with him. And when he rose in resurrection power, we were raised with him to walk in newness of life. Christ defeated sin's dominion at Calvary, then rose in triumph over sin, death, and hell. We now share in that victory as well as in the power that made it possible. Rebecca Manley Pippert wrote, "The very same power that raised Jesus from the dead, that made the amino acids rekindle and the corpse sit up, that revitalized dead cells and restored breath to empty lungs, is the power that is given to us when we receive Christ. Everything about the resurrection speaks of empowered newness."[18] So new creation has begun.

> Lives again our glorious King, Alleluia!
> Where, O death, is now thy sting? Alleluia!
> Once He died our souls to save, Alleluia!
> Where's thy victory, O grave? Alleluia!
>
> Soar we now where Christ hath led, Alleluia!
> Following our exalted Head, Alleluia!
> Made like Him, like Him we rise, Alleluia!
> Ours the cross, the grave, the skies, Alleluia![19]

11

With Jesus in the Heavens: *Ascension*

But God, being rich in mercy, because of the great love with
which he loved us, even when we were dead in our trespasses,
made us alive together with Christ—by grace you have been
saved—and raised us up with him and seated us with him in the
heavenly places in Christ Jesus.

Ephesians 2:4–6

A few years ago, I preached a series of sermons on the life of Jesus and
its saving significance for us, walking through the epochal events in
the life of Jesus as we approached Holy Week. After the resurrection
sermon on Easter Sunday, several people assumed the series was
finished. The notion was understandable, for while we preach on the
cross and resurrection often, we don't usually give much thought to
what happened next—Christ's ascension into heaven.

The ascension is a neglected doctrine. The apostles speak of
it often in the New Testament, but we don't speak about it often
enough in the church today.[1] And we are impoverished by this
neglect. John Owen, my favorite Puritan, wrote that the ascension
is essential to the church, "the great foundation of its hope and
consolation in this world."[2] He then concluded that "the darkness of
our faith herein is the cause of all our disconsolations, and most of

our weaknesses in obedience."[3] That's quite a statement. According to Owen, our spiritual unhappiness ("all our disconsolations") and faltering obedience are rooted in our neglect of the ascension. Why did Owen think the ascension is so important? Put simply, Christ's ascension into heaven is a pivotal event in the history of redemption. This is especially clear in Luke's writings. Luke wrote a two-part history of the origins of Christianity: volume one is the gospel that bears his name, and volume two is the book of Acts. The ascension was so important for Luke that he ended volume one with it (Luke 24:51), began volume two by reporting it again (Acts 1:9–11), and then referred to it multiple times in Acts. Because of this, Joel Green, a New Testament scholar who specializes in Luke's writings, concluded that for Luke, the one-two punch of resurrection and ascension are "*the* salvific event."[4]

The ascension also accounts for why Jesus ceased his post-resurrection appearances: he spent three days in the tomb, forty days resurrected, and then ascended to his throne. The ascension also foreshadowed the final event in salvific history—Jesus' personal, physical, glorious return. But there's more to the ascension than this. Christ's ascension was the necessary precursor to his ongoing ministry in, to, and through the church. In this chapter, we will reflect on five ways in which Jesus' ascension matters to the church today.

Jesus' Ascension and the Kingdom

Jesus' ascension to heaven and enthronement at God's right hand were the crowning events in his exaltation as king. Peter, preaching on the day of Pentecost, highlights how Jesus taking the throne fulfills Psalm 110 (Acts 2:33–36). Peter also sees the outpouring of the Holy Spirit as a direct consequence of Jesus' exaltation at God's right hand. Pentecost is therefore the public proof of Jesus' vindication and exaltation. The gift of the Spirit confirms the enthronement of the Son.

Of course, Jesus was always Israel's king. But like David between his anointing by Samuel and his actual coronation seven years later, Jesus kept his kingship somewhat hidden. This does not mean that Jesus never demonstrated his kingship during his earthly ministry (see Luke 11:20). But in his resurrection, ascension, and session, something unique took place. Now, he was *publicly invested* with all the kingly authority he already had by promise and by right. Now, "God has made him both Lord and Christ" (Acts 2:36). First "declared to be the Son of God in power according to the Spirit of holiness by his resurrection from the dead" (Rom. 1:4), Jesus now sits at God's "right hand in the heavenly places, far above all rule and authority and power and dominion, and above every name that is named, not only in this age but also in the one to come" (Eph. 1:20b–21). Jesus has taken the place of highest honor and reigns as the enthroned king.[5]

The Two States of Christ

Let's pause to define terms. In Christian theology, the *exaltation* of Christ is one of the two "states" of Christ. The other is the state of *humiliation*. We see these two states together in Philippians 2:8–9, "And being found in human form, he *humbled* himself by becoming obedient to the point of death, even death on a cross. Therefore God has highly *exalted* him and bestowed on him the name that is above every name."

These two states cover the whole of Jesus' humanity. The state of *humiliation* embraces his virginal conception, his humble birth, and his sinless life of perfect obedience under the law culminating in his agony, trial, suffering, and death. The state of *exaltation* commences with his resurrection, but also includes his ascension into heaven, his being seated at God's right hand (also called his *session*), and his glorious appearing. Then, he will come again to resurrect the dead, glorify the saints, judge the living and the dead, renew creation, and lead us into the eternal state where joy will never end and each day will be brighter than the one before.

This exaltation of Jesus now forms the foundation for the church's mission. Jesus said this when he gave the "great commission" in Matthew 28:

All authority in heaven and on earth has been given to me. Go therefore and make disciples of all nations, baptizing them in the name of the Father and of the Son and of the Holy Spirit, teaching them to observe all that I have commanded you. And behold, I am with you always, to the end of the age.

Matthew 28:18–20

Notice the "therefore" in verse 19. Why should we go and make disciples? *Because Jesus has been given "all authority in heaven and on earth."* The reason we make disciples, baptizing them in the three-fold name and teaching them to obey the commands of Jesus, is because Jesus has taken his seat as the exalted king. He is the world's true Lord.

This may explain why the book of Acts both begins and ends with references to Jesus' kingdom. Between his resurrection and ascension, Jesus "presented himself alive ... by many proofs, appearing to them during forty days and speaking about the kingdom of God" (Acts 1:3). On one such occasion, his disciples asked a question: "Lord, will you at this time restore the kingdom to Israel?" (v. 6). They still had a limited understanding of the kingdom. They still thought Jesus planned to restore the nation of Israel politically. Despite their misunderstanding, Jesus didn't rebuke them for asking the question, nor did he tell them that the kingdom was reserved for another age in the distant future. Instead, he reminded them that it's not for them to understand the Father's timing (v. 7), and he reassured them that they would receive the Spirit (v. 8). As soon as that happened (see Acts 2), the disciples became witnesses to Christ and his kingdom. In fact, the word "kingdom" pops up six more times in the book of Acts, each time in the context of proclamation, ending with Paul proclaiming the kingdom while under house arrest in Rome (Acts 8:12; 14:22; 19:8; 20:25; 28:23, 31).

Jesus and his kingdom remained a continuing reality for the early church. Far from indicating his departure from the church, his ascension means he maintains his connection to the church. Notice how Luke began the narrative in Acts by reminding Theophilus that he has already written of "all that Jesus *began* to do and teach" (Acts 1:1). This implies that Luke now writes of what Jesus *continues* to do and teach. The book of Acts isn't so much about the "Acts of the Apostles" (the work *they* did after Jesus left), but rather the continuing work of *Jesus* as our ascended and enthroned king through his Spirit-empowered church. The ascension of Christ as our king is therefore crucial to our ongoing consolation as his people. When tempted by discouragement amid our present, earthly sufferings, the ascension bids us turn our gaze upward to our risen king.

Jesus' Ascension and Pentecost

The ascension of Christ is not only the foundation of the church's mission; it is also the wellspring from which flow streams of power, encouragement, and comfort. For the exalted Jesus is the one who gives the church his Spirit to empower them for witness (Acts 1:8; 2:33). Jesus himself told his disciples that it was good for him to go away, because only then would he send them another Helper, the Spirit of truth: "I tell you the truth: it is to your advantage that I go away, for if I do not go away, the Helper will not come to you. But if I go, I will send him to you" (John 16:7).

> **Question 49:** How does Christ's ascension to heaven benefit us?
>
> **Answer:** First, he is our advocate in heaven in the presence of his Father. Second, we have our own flesh in heaven as a sure pledge that Christ our head will also take us, his members, up to himself. Third, he sends his Spirit to us on earth as a corresponding pledge. By the Spirit's power we seek not earthly things but the things above, where Christ is, sitting at God's right hand.
>
> —*The Heidelberg Catechism*

John had also written earlier in his gospel that the Spirit would come only after Jesus was glorified (John 7:39). And that is exactly what happened on the day of Pentecost, ten days after Jesus' ascension. The Spirit descended on the church with power, inaugurating a new age in salvation history. So significant was this moment that Bavinck wrote, "After the creation and the incarnation, the outpouring of the Spirit is the third great work of God."[6] But the catalyst of this outpouring was the ascension. That's why Peter connects Jesus' exaltation and the outpouring of the Spirit: "Being therefore exalted at the right hand of God, and having received from the Father the promise of the Holy Spirit, he has poured out this that you yourselves are seeing and hearing" (Acts 2:33). The ascension is the foundation of Pentecost.[7]

Indeed, Jesus' ascension was an integral event in redemptive history. Yes, salvation was *accomplished* when Jesus breathed his final breath on the cross and cried, "It is finished!" (John 19:30). But the salvation he accomplished must also be *applied*,[8] and that application is the work of the ascended Son through the agency of his descended Spirit. The old hymn writer captured this beautifully:

> He sends his Spirit from above,
> To call the objects of his love;
> Not one shall perish or be lost,
> His blood has bought them, dear they cost.[9]

By giving his Spirit, our exalted Lord makes the gospel effective, thus granting salvation to his people. "God exalted him at his right hand as Leader and Savior, to give repentance to Israel and forgiveness of sins" (Acts 5:31). Over and again in Acts, the "word of God" or "the word of the Lord" is said to increase, multiply, spread, or mightily prevail (6:7; 12:24; 13:49; 19:20). These references occur at key points in the narrative as Luke marks the progress of the word. And the fact that Luke uses "the word of God" and "the word of the Lord" interchangeably shows the functional equivalence of the Lord Jesus with God, thus highlighting Jesus' deity. The agency given to the word shows how Jesus accomplishes his divine purpose through the Spirit-anointed proclamation of the gospel.

In Acts we also witness how the ascended and enthroned Christ gives strength, courage, and comfort to his people through the Spirit as they bear witness to Jesus in the face of persecution and death. We especially see this in Stephen, the first martyr of the Christian church. After preaching that Jesus fulfilled redemptive history and replaced the temple, Stephen's hearers were enraged, ready to take his life. So they did, but in Acts 7:55–56, Luke tells us that Stephen, "full of the Holy Spirit, gazed into heaven and saw the glory of God, and Jesus standing at the right hand of God. And he said, 'Behold, I see the heavens opened, and the Son of Man standing at the right hand of God.'"

This should steel us with strength in our own missional efforts. When we lack courage and boldness, Luke reminds us that the exalted Christ has given us his Spirit, who equips us with power, boldness, and courage for mission. When we feel cynical about evangelism and think no one will respond to our message, or when we are tempted to resort to manipulative techniques, Luke reminds us that the exalted Christ is the Leader and Savior who grants repentance and forgiveness of sins. He is the King who seeks and saves the lost. That means we don't need to manipulate others and can nevertheless have confidence that some people will, in fact, respond. When we're paralyzed by fear of the risks involved in taking Jesus to hard-to-reach nations and neighborhoods, or when we feel threatened by rejection or persecution, Luke reminds us that the exalted Christ cares for his suffering people and stands to welcome the martyrs home.

Being filled with the Spirit isn't meant to be an *occasional* gift or blessing. Acts often describes the early Christians as being filled with the Spirit (2:4; 4:8, 31; 9:17; 13:9, 52). And Paul commands believers to continually be filled by the Spirit (Eph. 5:18). As John Stott writes, "The fullness of the Holy Spirit is emphatically not a privilege reserved for some, but a duty resting upon all."[10] The New Testament regularly presents the Spirit as the source of our spiritual life, the agent of our sanctification, the fountainhead of our power and joy and comfort, and both the initiator and sustainer of our union and communion with Christ and his church. The life of the Christian is life in the Spirit. To belong to Christ is to be indwelt by the Spirit. To be without the Spirit is to be without Christ (Rom. 8:9).

Jesus' Ascension and His Priesthood

Christ's ascension also means that he continues his priestly ministry for his people. This is deeply encouraging to struggling believers who doubt their security in God's grace. Paul assures us that no one can condemn those who are called and justified, precisely because of Christ's ongoing intercession. "Who is to condemn? Christ Jesus is the one who died—more than that, who was raised—who is at the right hand of God, who indeed is interceding for us."

The letter to the Hebrews, the only book in Scripture where Christ is directly called "priest," makes this continuing ministry rather plain. The writer declares how the eternal Son, the one whom God has "appointed the heir of all things, through whom also he created the world" and who is "the radiance of the glory of God and the exact imprint of his nature," who "upholds the universe by the word of his power," has now made "purification for sins," and has "sat down at the right hand of the Majesty on high" (Heb. 1:2–3). Over and again Hebrews emphasizes the ascension of Christ (see 4:14; 7:26; 8:1) so that we can see how Christ, as our great high priest, has now entered into the true sanctuary, the very presence of God himself, to appear before God on behalf of his people (9:24) and intercede for us (7:25). This is actually the consummation of Christ's priestly ministry[12] (Romans 8:34).

Spiritual Ascension, Trinitarian Communion

John Owen was Trinitarian through and through, and he left us a masterpiece of Trinitarian spirituality entitled *Of Communion with God the Father, Son, and Holy Ghost, Each Person Distinctly, in Love, Grace, and Consolation: Or, the Saints' Fellowship with the Father, Son, and Holy Ghost Unfolded.* Here, Owen wanted to show how the purpose of God's gracious plan was to "glorify the whole Trinity." So he described the believer's relationship with God in terms of "ascending to the Father's love through the work of the Spirit and blood of the Son."

What does that mean? It means that the Father is the fountain of divine love, and that his love is carried to us through the Son and then communicated to us by the Spirit. So our communion with God "is first by the work of the Spirit, to an actual interest in the blood of the Son; whence we have acceptation with the Father." The Spirit applies the work of Jesus to sinners and gives us a stake in the Divine Dance.

Thus we see the whole pattern of Christ's descent and ascent worked out in the believing experience of every Christian. Love descends from the Father through the Son in history and into our hearts by the Spirit. Our love returns along the same path: ascending by the Spirit, through the Son, and back to the Father again.[11]

John expresses a similar thought in slightly different words: "My little children, I am writing these things to you so that you may not sin. But if anyone does sin, we have an advocate with the Father, Jesus Christ the righteous. He is the propitiation for our sins, and not for ours only but also for the sins of the whole world" (1 John 2:1–2). John uses legal language (calling Jesus our advocate) instead of priestly language (noting how he intercedes), but the meaning is essentially the same. The wounds Christ yet retains in his glorified body forever testify: "'Forgive him, O forgive,' they cry, / 'Nor let that ransomed sinner die!'"[13] His ongoing role as our advocate and intercessor assures us that our sins are and shall be forgiven.

Do you understand, dear believer, what the priestly intercession of Christ means? It means that *Jesus is praying for you right now.* He knows your temptations, your weaknesses, your sins. He sees you faltering in the heat of the battle. He knows how discouraged you sometimes get. He knows, cares, and intercedes, continually presenting to the Father the merits of his saving accomplishments, the absolute sufficiency of his atoning death. That is why we can confidently sing,

> Before the throne of God above
> I have a strong and perfect plea;
> A great High Priest whose name is Love,
> Who ever lives and pleads for me.
> My name is graven on His hands,
> My name is written on His heart.
> I know that while in heav'n He stands,
> No tongue can bid me thence depart.
>
> When Satan tempts me to despair
> And tells me of the guilt within,
> Upward I look and see Him there
> Who made an end of all my sin.
> Because the sinless Savior died,
> My sinful soul is counted free.
> For God the Just is satisfied
> To look on Him and pardon me.[14]

Jesus' Ascension and the Lord's Table

Have you ever wondered why Christians include a meal as a crucial and regular part of worship? Why do we celebrate the Lord's Supper? And what does it have to do with the ascension? We can answer these questions by considering some of the scriptural passages that tell us about this meal, along with some of the names that have been attached to it.

First, when we come to the Table, we remember the sacrifice of Christ. This is a *memorial meal*, eaten in remembrance of what the Lord Jesus has accomplished for us. As Paul reminds us, Jesus "took bread, and when he had given thanks, he broke it, and said, 'This is my body which is for you. Do this in remembrance of me.' In the same way also he took the cup, after supper, saying, 'This cup is the new covenant in my blood. Do this, as often as you drink it, in remembrance of me'" (1 Cor. 11:23b–25).

The meal had deep historical roots in the story of Israel, particularly in their exodus from Egypt. God had given Israel the Passover meal just before their exodus, and they continued to celebrate it annually as they remembered how God had passed over their sins. When Jesus instituted the meal we now celebrate, he was eating his last Passover meal with his disciples. Paul makes that connection when he says that Christ is "our Passover lamb" (1 Cor. 5:7). Just as Passover was a memorial meal for Israel, pointing them back to God's saving work on their behalf, so the Lord's Table is a memorial meal for believers today, reminding us of God's final saving work in the death and resurrection of Jesus Christ.

Secondly, we come to the Table to celebrate our unity in Christ's body and give thanks to the Lord for his grace. When the gospel writers narrate the story of the Last Supper, they note how Jesus blessed or gave thanks for the bread and wine that they shared (Matt. 26:26–28; Mark 14:22–24; Luke 22:17–20). The word for "blessing" or "thanks" in these passages is Greek verb *eucharisteō*, which explains why some call this meal the Eucharist. But the Eucharist isn't a solitary meal; it's one we share with others. Paul says, "The cup of blessing that we bless, is it not a participation in the blood of Christ? The bread that we break, is it not a participation in the body of Christ? Because there is one bread, we who are many are one body, for we all partake of the one bread" (1 Cor. 10:16–17). We don't take the elements alone, but together. And when we do, we affirm and celebrate our oneness: that we belong to the Lord and to one another. Our unity in the church is derived from our union with Christ.

It matters when we gather at the Lord's Table that the Christ to which we are united is the crucified, risen, *and ascended* Christ.

After all, the Table is a special means of remembering, enjoying, and deepening our communion with him as he yet lives and intercedes for us. Paul assumes this in the passage quoted above, using the word *koinōnia* (translated in the ESV as "participation," 1 Cor. 10:16) to name the special fellowship we enjoy with Christ. This is why we sometimes refer to the Lord's Supper as Communion.

It is not that we eat and drink the actual body and blood of Christ. Nor is it true that Jesus is *physically* present with us at the Lord's Table. On the contrary, the meal celebrates that he is physically *absent*: his incarnate, crucified, resurrected, and ascended body is in heaven at the right hand of God. But through his Spirit, Christ manifests his *spiritual* presence to us in a unique way when we take the cup and the bread by faith. This is how we have "communion" with him. In so doing, we give him thanks for his perfect and finished sacrifice for us and for how he bestows on us his sanctifying, hope-giving grace by giving us himself.

The Lord's Table, then, is a visible demonstration of our present union with Christ. We are not only crucified with Christ (Gal. 2:20), but are also raised and seated with him (Eph. 2:6; Col. 3:1;). As Gerrit Scott Dawson says in his insightful book *Jesus Ascended*, the Lord's Supper is a means of grace for experiencing this "spiritual ascension."

> At the table of grace, Jesus who is absent from us draws near by the work of the Holy Spirit. The elements do not literally become the body and blood of Jesus. But Jesus, who is still actually embodied, feeds us with the power, the energy and the virtue of his glorified life through the sacrament.... When we partake of the sacrament with faith that fixes on the reality of who Jesus is, we are lifted up into his presence and nourished by his very life.[15]

Dawson's perspective corresponds with Calvin's teaching on the Lord's Supper. For Calvin, the Table was more than just a memorial meal. It was a sacred supper through which Christ himself nourishes and strengthens believers with his glorified humanity. This is not to suggest that the meal mechanically transmits grace to an unbelieving heart. Nor does Christ descend to the Table. Instead, his Spirit raises our hearts to the heavens, so that we commune with the ascended

Savior.[16] Summarizing Calvin, Ronald Wallace thus writes, "Since we are creatures who must see with our eyes and handle with our hands, the Lord's Table is set before us in order that we may know that the ascended Christ is not separated from us."[17] We celebrate the Lord's Supper not only because it reminds us that Jesus broke his body and shed his blood for us, but also because he yet lives and intercedes for us.

Jesus' Ascension and our Humanity

Finally, when we consider Christ as our ascended and exalted king, we must never forget that *he ascended in his true incarnate and glorified humanity*. He did not leave his human nature behind when he ascended to the Father. We see this in Hebrews 2, where the author quotes from Psalm 8 to remind us of God's original purpose and intention for humanity to have dominion over the earth:

> It has been testified somewhere,
> "What is man, that you are mindful of him,
> or the son of man, that you care for him?
> You made him for a little while lower than the angels;
> you have crowned him with glory and honor,
> putting everything in subjection under his feet."
>
> Now in putting everything in subjection to him, he left nothing
> outside his control. At present, we do not yet see everything
> in subjection to him. But we see him who for a little while was
> made lower than the angels, namely Jesus, crowned with glory
> and honor because of the suffering of death, so that by the grace
> of God he might taste death for everyone.
>
> Hebrews 2:6–9

Down and Up Again

In his brilliant essay, "The Grand Miracle," C. S. Lewis uses the picture of a diver to illustrate the whole story of Christ's descent and ascent—both his humiliation and exaltation.

"The story of the Incarnation is the story of a descent and a resurrection. When I say 'resurrection' here, I am not referring simply to the first few hours, or the first few weeks of the Resurrection. I am talking of this whole, huge pattern of descent, down, down, and then up again. What we ordinarily call the Resurrection being just, so to speak, the point at which it turns. Think what that descent is. The coming down, not only into humanity, but into those nine months which precede human birth ... and going lower still into being a corpse, a thing which, if this ascending movement had not begun, would presently have passed out of the organic altogether, and have gone back into the inorganic, as all corpses do.... One has the picture of a diver, stripping off garment after garment, making himself naked, then flashing for a moment in the air, and then down through the green, and warm, and sunlit water into the pitch black, cold, freezing water, down into the mud and slime, then up again, his lungs almost bursting, back again to the green and warm and sunlit water, and then at last out into the sunshine, holding in his hand the dripping thing he went down to get. This thing is human nature; but, associated with it, all nature, the new universe."[18]

Lewis is showing us how Christ, by descending in humility and ascending in glory, has redeemed human nature, but also the whole created order. In the resurrection and ascension of Jesus, we see the redemption, exaltation, and glorification of human nature itself.

God planned in creation to place all things under the feet of man. But when we look around now, we see nothing of the sort. "At present, we do *not* yet see everything in subjection to him" (v. 8c). Birds destroy crops. Insects spread diseases. Wild animals maim and kill human beings. The natural world seems "red in tooth and claw."[19] Human beings fight for their survival, eking a living out of the earth through blood, sweat, and toil.

But in verse 9, we read about Jesus "who for a little while was made lower than the angels ... crowned with glory and honor because of the suffering of death, so that by the grace of God he might taste death for everyone." Why does the author apply Psalm 8 to Jesus? Because Jesus, having tasted the suffering of death, has vanquished the power of death itself (vv. 14–15), and is now "crowned with glory and honor" in his glorified human nature. This means that humanity, through Jesus of Nazareth our exalted and enthroned king, has resumed its lordship over creation. As the old Scottish professor John Duncan said, "The Dust of the Earth is on the throne of the Majesty on High."[20]

By descending in humility and ascending in glory, Christ has redeemed human nature—indeed, the entire created order. In the resurrection and ascension of Jesus, we see the redemption, exaltation, and glorification of human nature itself. The second Adam reigns! And if you are in Christ, you reign with him.

> He has raised our human nature
> On the clouds to God's right hand;
> There we sit in heav'nly places,
> There with Him in glory stand.
> Jesus reigns, adored by angels;
> Man with God is on the throne;
> By our mighty Lord's ascension
> We by faith behold our own.[21]

12

With Jesus in Glory: *Return*

When Christ who is your life appears, then you also will appear
with him in glory.

Colossians 3:4

When I was eleven years old, my family took a two-week trip west,
traveling by car from West Texas all the way to California. My dad
preached in a California church over the first weekend, followed by
a two-day stay in Anaheim where we visited Disneyland. This was
my first trip to Disneyland, so I had big expectations. But I was old
enough to have started thinking seriously about spiritual matters. I
will never forget lying awake the night before going to Disneyland
hoping and praying that Jesus wouldn't return the next morning!

This, I think, is a picture of how many people think about the
second coming of Christ. We want him to come back ... but not yet.
First, we want to go to Disneyland—or college, or Europe. We want
to get married, or have children, or grandchildren. Then, after we've
had the best this life can offer, maybe we'll be ready to meet Jesus.

But when we read the New Testament and consider the
perspective of the early Christians on the return of Christ, we get
quite a different picture. They longed to see Christ appear (Titus 2:13).
Several passages describe believers waiting "eagerly" for our future

hope (Rom. 8:19, 23; Gal. 5:5; Heb. 9:28). Paul also exhorted believers to encourage one another with the doctrine of Christ's future return (1 Thess. 4:18; 5:11).

Why do some believers feel indifferent about the return of Christ? Some, perhaps, are not truly regenerate and are Christian in name only. Others find discussions of eschatology confusing, maybe even scary. Many believers are poorly informed with what Scripture actually says about the future, with beliefs shaped more by *Left Behind* or apocalyptic movies than by the apostolic word. To be sure, some parts of Scripture are difficult to interpret—take the book of Revelation, for example. The strangeness of the biblical literature and the variety of confusing interpretations can leave even studious Christians feeling intimidated. For these reasons and more, we are largely uninformed about biblical teaching. And we do not think much about that which we do not know.

But the hope of Christ's return is integral to Christian faith. The story of Christ and his people is incomplete without it. Our failure to give attention to the second coming means that we impoverish both others and ourselves. Moreover, this doctrine is good news for all who are united to Christ. As Paul writes to the saints at Colossae, "When Christ who is your life appears, then you also will appear *with him* in glory" (Col. 3:4). This is true for all who have died and been raised with Christ, whose life is hidden with Christ in God (vv. 1–3). Indeed, those who are predestined, called, and justified are also glorified (Rom. 8:30). It makes sense, therefore, to bring our study to a close by looking forward to the day when we will be with Jesus in glory. In this chapter we will look at four distinct but related aspects of the Christian hope: the second advent of Christ, the resurrection of the body, the day of judgment, and the creation of a new heavens and new earth.

The Second Advent of Christ

Interestingly enough, the language of "second coming" is rather sparse in the New Testament. Jesus told his disciples, "If I go and prepare a place for you, I will come again and will take you to myself, that where I am you may be also" (John 14:3). And the writer to the Hebrews describes how Christ "will appear a second time, not to deal with sin but to save those who are eagerly waiting for him" (Heb. 9:28). The phrase "second coming" is certainly not a misnomer, then, but the Scriptures speak of Christ's second advent with other words as well, such as simply "coming" (*parousia*), but also "appearing" (*epiphaneia*), "appears" (*phaneroō*), and "revelation" (*apokalypsis*). Let's think more about what these words mean.

The word *parousia* simply means "presence." When translated "It does not usually connote the idea of returning but in this context assumes that Jesus, having been "absent and hidden for a time ... and having then come back ... will again be and remain present."[1] Paul uses this word often in 1 Thessalonians. For example, he asks, "What is our hope or joy or crown of boasting before our Lord Jesus at his coming? Is it not you?" (2:19). He then prays that God "may establish your hearts blameless in holiness before our God and Father, at the coming of our Lord Jesus with all his saints" (3:13). He also reminds them that those "who are alive, who are left until the coming of the Lord, will not precede those who have fallen asleep," for "the dead in Christ will rise first" (4:15–16). Finally, Paul commends his readers with this blessing: "Now may the God of peace himself sanctify you completely, and may your whole spirit and soul and body be kept blameless at the coming of our Lord Jesus Christ" (5:23). Paul continues to describe the coming of Christ as *parousia* in 2 Thessalonians (2:1, 8, 9), and other apostles use this word as well (James 5:7–8; 2 Peter 1:16; 3:4; 1 John 2:28).

More vivid than *parousia* is the word *epiphaneia*, for this word stresses the visible manifestation of Christ. In 2 Timothy 1:10, Paul uses *epiphaneia* to describe Christ's *first* advent, saying that God's purpose and grace "has been manifested through the *appearing* of our Savior Christ Jesus who abolished death and brought life and immortality to light through the gospel." But he also uses the word four times in the Pastoral Epistles to reference the *future* appearing of Christ in his second advent. For example, Titus 2:13 describes "our blessed hope, the appearing of the glory of our great

God and Savior Jesus Christ" (see also 1 Tim. 6:14; 2 Tim. 4:1, 8). Some interpreters of Scripture believe that the *parousia* and *epiphaneia* refer to two distinct events: the first a secret rapture of the church, the second a public appearing to the world. But it is significant that Paul uses the words *epiphaneia* and *parousia* together in 2 Thessalonians 2:8 when he speaks of the Lord Jesus and "the appearance of his coming." This indicates that to Paul, the two words describe a single event: the visible and public appearing of Christ.[2]

Similar in meaning is the word *phaneroō*, a verb meaning "to appear." Paul uses this word twice in Colossians 3:4, writing "When Christ who is your life *appears*, then you also will *appear* with him in glory." Similarly, Peter reminds the elders that they will receive an unfading crown of glory "when the Chief Shepherd *appears*" (1 Peter 5:4), while the apostle John writes, "And now, little children, abide in him, so that when he *appears* we may have confidence and not shrink from him in shame at his coming" (1 John 2:28). The word for *coming* at the end of that verse is the word *parousia*, which we have already considered.

The fourth word used in the New Testament for Christ's second advent is *apokalypsis*, from which we get our word *apocalypse*. This word is sometimes translated "revelation" and indicates an "unveiling." In the words of Louis Berkhof, "It points to the uncovering of something that was previously hidden from view, in this case, of the concealed glory and majesty of Jesus Christ."[3] This is the word Peter uses when he says that the tried and tested faith of the saints will be "found to result in praise and glory and honor at the *revelation* of Jesus Christ" (1 Peter 1:7; cf. 1:13; 4:13). Paul speaks of waiting "for the *revealing* of Jesus Christ" (1 Cor. 1:7) and anticipates the day "when the Lord Jesus is *revealed* from heaven with his mighty angels" (2 Thess. 1:7).

Taken alongside other passages associated with the second coming (e.g., Acts 1:9–11; 3:19–21; Rev. 1:7), these terms describe an event that will be personal, physical, public, and visible. The second advent of Christ will be witnessed not only by the church, but by the whole world. And this event will bring salvation to the faithful, judgment to the wicked, and restoration to the entire created order.

The Resurrection of the Body

Every Sunday, thousands of believers around the world together say the Apostles' Creed and confess, "I believe ... in the resurrection of the body." Christianity is a resurrection religion, with the bodily resurrection of Jesus Christ the foundation of our hope. But as we saw in chapter 10, Christ's resurrection was the firstfruits of the future resurrection (1 Cor. 15:20, 23). He is the firstborn from the dead (Col. 1:18; Rev. 1:5), the "pioneer" of our salvation (Heb. 2:10, NRSV). His rising from the dead was but the first movement in the grand symphony of resurrection yet to come. Our eschatological hope therefore anticipates the future and final resurrection of the body.

Paul spells this out for the Corinthians:

> But in fact Christ has been raised from the dead, the firstfruits
> of those who have fallen asleep. For as by a man came death,
> by a man has come also the resurrection of the dead. For as in
> Adam all die, so also in Christ shall all be made alive. But each
> in his own order: Christ the firstfruits, then at his coming those
> who belong to Christ. Then comes the end, when he delivers the
> kingdom to God the Father after destroying every rule and every
> authority and power.
>
> 1 Corinthians 15:20–24

Once more we see Jesus as the second Adam, the new man who brings resurrection to all "who belong to Christ."

The Scriptures also describe the resurrection of all people, righteous and wicked alike. We see this in John 5, where Jesus says, "Do not marvel at this, for an hour is coming when all who are in the tombs will hear his voice and come out, those who have done good to the resurrection of life, and those who have done evil to the resurrection of judgment" (vv. 28–29). Revelation 20 gives a similar picture, describing the resurrection of the martyrs (v. 4) followed by a general resurrection (v. 5). These passages echo Daniel 12:2, one of the few references to resurrection in the Old Testament, where "many of those who sleep in the dust of the earth shall awake, some to everlasting life, and some to shame and everlasting contempt." Paul also confessed his hope in the future "resurrection of both the just and the unjust" in Acts 24:15.

But the New Testament primarily focuses on the resurrection of believers. Paul says that when the Lord descends from heaven, "the dead in Christ will rise first" (1 Thess. 4:16). Elsewhere, he reminds us that "if we have been united with him in a death like his, we shall certainly be united with him in a resurrection like his" (Rom. 6:5). It is in this final resurrection that we will finally receive "the redemption of our bodies" (Rom. 8:23). This resurrection will happen concurrently with glorification, the moment when Jesus "will transform our lowly body to be like his glorious body" (Phil. 3:21), when "this perishable body must put on the imperishable, and this mortal body must put on immortality" (1 Cor. 15:53; cf. 1 John 3:2). As Bavinck explains:

> This is the real, the true resurrection won directly by Christ, for it is not just a reunion of soul and body, but also an act of vivification, a renewal. It is an event in which believers, united in soul and body, enter into communion with Christ and are being re-created after God's image (Rom. 8:11, 29; Phil. 3:21). For that reason Paul has the resurrection of believers coincide with the transformation of those who are left alive. The latter will have no advantage over the former, for the resurrection will take place prior to the transformation, and together they will go forth to meet the Lord in the air (1 Cor. 15:51–52; 2 Cor. 5:2, 4; 1 Thess. 4:15–17).[4]

And it is Christ's resurrection that guarantees ours.

Near the end of C. S. Lewis's Narnian adventure *The Silver Chair*, in a chapter called "The Healing of Harms," the children Jill and Eustace somehow begin to hear music for King Caspian's funeral as they walk with Aslan on his mountain. They walk beside a stream, Aslan going before them, "and he became so beautiful, and the music so despairing, that Jill did not know which of them it was that filled her eyes with tears." Then the lion stops. And when the children look into the stream, they see the body of King Caspian. All three of them—Jill, Eustace, and Aslan—weep. Then Aslan tells Eustace to find a thorn in a nearby thicket....

> Eustace obeyed. The thorn was a foot long and sharp as a rapier.
> "Drive it into my paw, Son of Adam," said Aslan, holding up his right fore-paw and spreading out the great pad toward Eustace.
> "Must I?" said Eustace.
> "Yes," said Aslan.
> Then Eustace set his teeth and drove the thorn into the Lion's pad. And there came out a great drop of blood, redder than all redness that you have ever seen or imagined. And it splashed into the stream over the dead body of the King. At the same moment the doleful music stopped. And the dead King began to be changed. His white beard turned to grey, and from grey to yellow, and got shorter and vanished altogether; and his sunken cheeks grew round and fresh, and the wrinkles were smoothed, and his eyes opened, and his eyes and lips both laughed, and suddenly he leaped up and stood before them—a very young man, or a boy.[5]

Attentive readers will remember that Aslan himself had suffered death and resurrection earlier in Narnian history. Now it is the virtuous power of Aslan's blood that restores life and youth to the deceased king. In like manner, our future resurrection is connected to the resurrection of Christ, who is "the firstfruits of those who have fallen asleep" (1 Cor. 15:20) and "the firstborn from the dead" (Col. 1:18). "For if we have been united with him in a death like his, we shall certainly be united with him in a resurrection like his" (Rom. 6:5).

The Day of Judgment

In the Apostles' Creed we also confess, "He shall come to judge the quick and the dead." Here, "quick" refers to the living, not the really fast! So we confess that Jesus will one day judge both those alive at that moment of judgment and those who have already died.

When will this happen? Theologians remain somewhat divided on the exact timing of this judgment, but the fact of judgment itself could not be clearer in Scripture. As Peter says in Acts 10:42, "[Jesus] commanded us to preach to the people and to testify that he is the one appointed by God to be judge of the living and the dead." Paul uses the same language in 2 Timothy: "I charge you in the presence of God and of Christ Jesus, who is to judge the living and the dead, and by his appearing and his kingdom: preach the word" (4:1–2a). In another letter, he writes, "We must all appear before the judgment seat of Christ, so that each one may receive what is due for what he has done in the body, whether good or evil" (2 Cor. 5:10). And in the book of Revelation, we read about the "great white throne" of judgment, where the books are opened and the "dead [are] judged by what was written in the books, according to what they had done" (20:11–12).

Jesus spoke frequently about the day of judgment, warning people that Sodom and Gomorrah would find the day of judgment more tolerable than they would (Matt. 10:15). Jesus' warnings are both serious and urgent. "I tell you, on the day of judgment people will give account for every careless word they speak, for by your words you will be justified, and by your words you will be condemned" (Matt. 12:36–37). And in John 5, Jesus connects the final judgment to the resurrection of the body, declaring that the Father has entrusted judgment to him as the Son of Man:

> Truly, truly, I say to you, whoever hears my word and believes
>   him who sent me has eternal life. He does not come into
>   judgment, but has passed from death to life.
> Truly, truly, I say to you, an hour is coming, and is now here,
>   when the dead will hear the voice of the Son of God, and those
>   who hear will live. For as the Father has life in himself, so he
>   has granted the Son also to have life in himself. And he has
>   given him authority to execute judgment, because he is the
>   Son of Man. Do not marvel at this, for an hour is coming when
>   all who are in the tombs will hear his voice and come out,
>   those who have done good to the resurrection of life, and those
>   who have done evil to the resurrection of judgment.
>
> John 5:24–29

The scriptural testimony is clear. There will be a day of judgment: a day in which all people, living and dead, righteous and wicked, will give an account of their words and deeds to the living God. This judgment will be final and irrevocable, leading to one of two destinies— either everlasting life or everlasting punishment. Reflecting on future judgment can therefore be both encouraging and threatening.

The day of judgment is encouraging because it means we will see justice in the world. There will be a day of reckoning.

> **Question 52:** How does Christ's return "to judge the living and the dead" comfort you?
>
> **Answer:** In all distress and persecution, with uplifted head, I confidently await the very judge who has already offered himself to the judgment of God in my place and removed the whole curse from me. Christ will cast all his enemies and mine into everlasting condemnation, but will take me and all his chosen ones to himself into the joy and glory of heaven.
>
> —*The Heidelberg Catechism*

Wickedness will not go unpunished. This assurance is especially important for the persecuted, abused, and oppressed peoples of the world. As an analogy, consider the importance of retribution for storybook villains. Remember, for example, Hansel and Gretel. Tricked by a witch and destined to become her supper, they end up escaping only after they shove her into her own oven and run away. You may find this story scary and likely to upset children, but in his wise book about literature, Gene Edward Veith argues the opposite. Children are often victims of injustice, whether small or big, and have an innate longing for retribution. So when injustice goes unpunished, children feel unprotected. Far from producing anxiety, the punishment of villains in fairy tales provides children with a sense of security.[6]

When the Bible forecasts future divine judgment for the wicked, the persecuted, abused, and oppressed find themselves similarly comforted. When we are treated wrongly, we long for justice. If our desire for justice has no regard for God as supreme judge, it quickly morphs into vengeance. But when placed within the locus of God's justice, this longing fits into the reality of a morally ordered universe. Robbing Christianity of the doctrine of future judgment robs suffering people of the very resource they need if they will move forward in faith and perseverance, not shackled by bitterness or the quest for personal vengeance.

But the doctrine of future judgment is also threatening. Why? Because we know we are guilty. Nothing is more terrifying than the guarantee that "God will bring every deed into judgment, with every secret thing, whether good or evil" (Eccl. 12:14). We know we have sinned. If we're honest, we must confess with Shakespeare's King Richard, "My conscience hath a thousand several tongues, / And every tongue brings in a several tale, / And every tale condemns me for a villain."[7] Each of us, therefore, faces this one great question: how will I stand in the day of judgment?

We find the answer in the gospel, the good news that the Judge is also the Redeemer. And having come to rescue us from coming wrath, he will not now abandon us.[8] This really is good news! You *can* stand in judgment because the Judge has already taken judgment in your place. He was condemned that you might be acquitted. Dear Christian, the gospel assures you that your verdict has already been pronounced: *Not guilty!* "Who shall bring any charge against God's elect? It is God who justifies. Who is to condemn? Christ Jesus is the one who died—more than that, who was raised—who is at the right hand of God, who indeed is interceding for us" (Rom. 8:33–34).

The only fitting response to such grace is worship! We can sing thus with John Newton:

> Let us wonder, grace and justice
> Join and point to mercy's store;
> When through grace in Christ our trust is,
> Justice smiles, and asks no more;
> He who wash'd us in his blood
> Has secured our way to God.[9]

Grace Restores Nature

Herman Bavinck towers head and shoulders above most theologians, though he is only beginning to be more widely read in English. His chief accomplishment was the four-volume masterpiece *Gereformeerde Dogmatiek*, originally published in Dutch between 1895 and 1899. The English translation, *Reformed Dogmatics*, was completed in 2008 and is a treasure trove of theological reflection that I've quoted often in this book.

The melody running through all four movements of Bavinck's theological symphony is the happy theme that "grace restores nature." In Bavinck's own words, "Grace serves, not to take up humans into a supernatural order, but to free them from sin. Grace is opposed not to nature, only to sin .... Grace restores nature and takes it to its highest pinnacle."[10] Bavinck understood that God's ultimate purpose is not to rescue human beings from the created world by releasing us from our bodies and relocating us to heaven, but rather to renew the fallen creation and reestablish God's kingdom on earth, with human beings as his restored image-bearers. The goal, then, is not escape, but recreation, renewal, and redemption. Bavinck cited Christ's resurrection as the greatest proof for this claim: "The bodily resurrection of Christ from the dead is conclusive proof that Christianity does not adopt a hostile attitude towards anything human or natural, but intends only to deliver creation from all that is sinful, and to sanctify it completely."[11]

Thus, when it comes to eschatology, Bavinck looked for the "renewal of the world ... [which] is never a second, brand-new creation but a re-creation of the existing world. God's honor consists precisely in the fact that he redeems and renews the same humanity, the same world, the same heaven, and the same earth that have been corrupted and polluted by sin. Just as anyone in Christ is a new creation in whom the old has passed away and everything has become new (2 Cor. 5:17), so also this world passes away in its present form as well, in order out of its womb, at God's Word of power, to give birth and being to a new world."[12] In fact, the final chapter of Bavinck's four-volume project is entitled "The Renewal of Creation."

I think Bavinck would have agreed with the hymnist Isaac Watts:

> No more let sins and sorrows grow,
> Nor thorns infest the ground;
> He comes to make his blessings flow
> Far as the curse is found.[13]

The New Heavens and New Earth

We wait for Christ's glorious return, the resurrection of the body, and the final judgment, but the Christian hope does not end there. To quote the Apostles' Creed once more, we also believe in "the life everlasting." Some imagine that our spirits will float on clouds, existing in a kind of lazy joy forever, but the Scriptures nowhere present eternal life as an ethereal, immaterial existence. The very bodies raised and transformed in glory will live in a material environment that is also glorified, redeemed, and restored. This is why we "rejoice in hope of the glory of God" (Rom. 5:2) as we "wait eagerly" with the creation itself for "the freedom of the glory of the children of God" and our "adoption as sons, the redemption of our bodies" (Rom. 8:21, 23).

This is the renewal of all things Jesus described in Matthew 19:28, the restoration Peter proclaimed in Acts 3:21, the cosmic unification Paul anticipated in Ephesians 1:10, and the new creation Isaiah prophesied in Isaiah 65–66. All things will be renewed and restored in Christ, united together under his reign and recreated by his almighty power, thus reversing once and for all the effects of the fall and instating human beings for all time in "a new earth in which righteousness dwells" (2 Peter 3:13). The desert will blossom like the rose (Isa. 35:1), the river of God will water the earth, bringing life and joy in its flow (Ezek. 47), the wolf will lie with the lamb (Isa. 11:6), and the earth will be filled with the glory of God as the waters cover the sea (Isa. 11:9). This is the return to Eden, the reunion of heaven and earth. Paradise will be regained!

One of the most glorious depictions of this in all of Scripture is found in the last two chapters of Scripture, where John describes the city of God descending from heaven to earth. They deserve much re-reading, but these brief excerpts can help us consider specifically what union with Christ means for that glorious age to come:

> Then I saw a new heaven and a new earth, for the first heaven
> and the first earth had passed away, and the sea was no more.
> And I saw the holy city, new Jerusalem, coming down out of
> heaven from God, prepared as a bride adorned for her husband.

And I heard a loud voice from the throne saying, "Behold, the dwelling place of God is with man. He will dwell with them, and they will be his people, and God himself will be with them as their God. He will wipe away every tear from their eyes, and death shall be no more, neither shall there be mourning, nor crying, nor pain anymore, for the former things have passed away."

And he who was seated on the throne said, "Behold, I am making all things new."

Revelation 21:1–5a

Then the angel showed me the river of the water of life, bright as crystal, flowing from the throne of God and of the Lamb through the middle of the street of the city; also, on either side of the river, the tree of life with its twelve kinds of fruit, yielding its fruit each month. The leaves of the tree were for the healing of the nations.

Revelation 22:1–2

The picture is mysterious, evocative, powerful, stunning. With language reminiscent of Eden, John portrays a vision of the world to come brimming with life, beauty, glory, and joy. We will inhabit a world so familiar, but altogether new. What humanity and the whole of creation have lost through sin will now be regained, renewed, and restored.

This is the end of the beginning. And it is the beginning of the never-ending story, the final state of everlasting joy and gladness, peace and prosperity, and bounty and blessing for God's people. This marks the fulfillment of God's grand covenant promise to make his home on earth, to reside once more with human beings. God will make his dwelling place with us. God will be eternally glorified. We will be everlastingly satisfied, bursting with praise and overflowing in joy.

There we will know, once and for all, the ceasing of our sorrows, the banishment of our tears, the healing of all harms, the reversal of death itself. There, all the hurts of this world will be healed once and for all, wholeness will be restored, beauty will be eternal, faith will be sight, and everything sad will become untrue.[14] Death will be swallowed up forever. God himself will reign. And we will feast at the banqueting table of our Savior and Redeemer.

"And so we will always be with the Lord" (1 Thess 4:17).

Notes

Epigraph

1. Martin, *Christ for Us*, 49–50.

Introduction

1. Tolkien, *Two Towers*, 321.

2. For an insightful article comparing and contrasting the *ordo salutis* (order of salvation) and the *historia salutis* (history of salvation) along with two other models for understanding salvation, see Frame, "Salvation and Theological Pedagogy."

3. Murray, *Redemption*, 170. See also contemporary Reformed theologian Robert Letham's *Union with Christ*.

4. This subject of covenant is one that fuels intramural debate among theologians. The disagreements that exist among the various camps are not relevant to this particular book, but for further reading, consider Horton, *Introducing Covenant Theology*; Gentry and Wellum, *Kingdom through Covenant*; and Williamson, *Sealed with an Oath*.

5. Ferguson, *Christian Life*, 108.

6. In theological language, baptism does not work in *ex opere operato* (Latin, "from the work worked"). In other words, the sacrament is neither magical nor mechanical. Rather, as the Westminster Confession of Faith states, "The grace which is exhibited in or by the sacraments rightly used, is not conferred by any power in them; neither does the efficacy of a sacrament depend upon the piety or intention of him that does administer it: but upon the work of the Spirit, and the word of institution, which contains, together with a precept authorizing the use thereof, a promise of benefit to worthy receivers" (27.3).

7. Ferguson, *Christian Life*, 109.

8. Ibid., 107.

9. Calvin, *Institutes*, 3.2.24.

10. I've written an entire book devoted to developing this theme. See Hedges, *Christ Formed in You*.

11. Letham draws this out as well: "Not only does our union with Christ have external aspects, but it also transforms us from within. When Christ died and rose from the dead, we died and rose with him, and so our status and existence was dramatically changed. Since, following Christ's ascension, the Holy Spirit was sent to bring us to spiritual life and indwell and renew us, our participation in Christ's death and resurrection is vitally dynamic and transformative. These two elements are inseparable" (*Union with Christ*, 85).

12. See Hedges, *Christ Formed in You*, chapter 5.

13. For the overall structure of this book, I am partially indebted to a series of sermons preached jointly by Sinclair B. Ferguson and Derek W. H. Thomas at First Presbyterian Church in Columbia, South Carolina, in 2013. I listened to most of these sermons while preparing my own messages in 2014 and only near the end of writing *With Jesus* did I discover that the sermons had been published in a volume entitled *Ichthus: Jesus Christ, God's Son, the Saviour*. Readers who compare their expositions with mine will see both how their series influenced me and also how I took some different paths.

Chapter 1. With Jesus in the Manger: Birth

1. Stapert, *Handel's Messiah*, especially 41–45, 53.

2. Charles Jennens, who compiled the passages to form the *Messiah* libretto, sent Handel words to preface the *Messiah*, and those words came from 1 Timothy 3:16 and Colossians 2:3 (ibid., 42, 85). Others have found the incarnation worthy of song as well. Consider, for example, this verse from "Hark, the Herald Angels Sing," a Christmas carol by Charles Wesley:

Veiled in flesh the Godhead see
Hail incarnate deity
Pleased on earth with man to dwell
Jesus our Immanuel.

3. Bavinck, *Reformed Dogmatics*, 3:274.

4. "The basis of our union with Christ is Christ's union with us in the incarnation. We can become one with him because he first became one with us. By taking human nature into personal union, the Son of God has joined himself to humanity," writes Letham (*Union with Christ*, 21). Indeed, "The complete identification of the eternal Son with our flesh and blood is part of our union with him" (41).

5. Garland, *Luke*, 121.

6. The Chalcedonian Creed. Quoted in Allison, *Historical Theology*, 376–377. I highly recommend Allison's concise discussion of how the Chalcedonian Creed explicitly denied various earlier heresies with specific wording against their major tenets.

7. "The maker of man, he was made man, so that the director of the stars might be a babe at the breast; that bread might be hungry, and the fountain thirsty; that the light might sleep, and the way be weary from a journey; that the truth might be accused by false witnesses, and the judge of the living and the dead be judged by a mortal judge; that justice might be convicted by the unjust, and discipline be scourged with whips; that the cluster of the grapes might be crowned with thorns, and the foundation be hung up on a tree; that strength might grow weak, eternal health be wounded, life die." Augustine, Sermon 191, 42.

8. "God wished His Son to be circumcised that He might come under the Law. . . . So Christ by receiving circumcision professed Himself a servant of the Law, to win us our freedom." Calvin, *Calvin's New Testament Commentaries*, 1:81.

9. Owen, *Meditations and Discourses*, 339.

10. Throughout this book, you will notice questions and answers from the Heidelberg Catechism articulating the truths explored in the main text. The version quoted here is that approved by the Christian Reformed Church in 1975, available online at https://www.rca.org/heidelberg.

11. Bock, *Luke 1:1–9:50*, 122.

12. Letham, *Union with Christ*, 41. We also sing this great truth in hymns like Charles Wesley's "Come, Desire of Nations, Come."

13. Smith, "Gospel Genre."

14. Bowley, "Pax Romana," 773.

15. Edwards, "Dissertation I," 405–536.

16. Plantinga, *Not the Way*, 10.

Chapter 2. With Jesus in the River: Baptism

1. Carson, *Matthew*, 107. See also Osborne, *Matthew*, 122.

2. "The word 'fulfill,' normally used by Matthew in his quotation formula in connection with the completion of a scripturally authenticated pattern . . . suggests that this baptism has a role in the carrying out of Jesus' specific mission." France, *Gospel of Matthew*, 120.

3. Calvin, *Calvin's New Testament Commentaries*, 1:129–130.

4. Ferguson and Thomas highlighted the biblical-theological connections between baptism and judgment (see 1 Cor. 10:1–2; 1 Peter 3:18–22): "John's baptism then was a kind of declaration of war against the sins of God's people because they had violated his covenant. . . . John's baptism is a clarion call for repentance. John stands as the prosecuting counsel; he now presents a divine lawsuit against his contemporaries. For God is declaring a judgment against them as catastrophic as the Flood in the time of Noah or as the drowning of the Egyptians in the time of Moses" (*Ichthus*, 26).

5. "At the very beginning of Jesus' public ministry, his Father presented him, in a veiled way, as at once Davidic Messiah, very Son of God, representative of the people, and Suffering Servant. Matthew has already introduced all these themes and will develop them further." Carson, *Matthew*, 109.

6. Quoted in Green, *Message of Matthew*, 81.

7. Owen, *Pneumatologia*, 152–188.

8. "Jesus does not resort to his divine nature in order to accomplish what needs to be done in our human nature. No. Were he to do that, he would no longer be the second man, the last Adam. He would no longer be our representative," write Ferguson and Thomas. "What then accounts for Jesus' faithfulness to God? The answer is that from the beginning to the end of his life he was empowered and strengthened in his human nature by the Holy Spirit" (*Ichthus*, 30).

9. Gregory of Nazianzus, "To Cledonius the Priest," 440. Gregory contended that the views of Apollinarius of Laodicea (who believed that Jesus had a human body, but not a human mind) compromised our salvation.

10. Ferguson, *Holy Spirit*, 37.

11. Calvin, *Calvin's New Testament Commentaries*, 1:132–133.

12. "The bearer of the Spirit becomes the bestower of the Spirit." Cole, *He Who Gives Life*, 179.

Chapter 3. *With Jesus in the Desert: Temptation*

1. "It is difficult to be certain exactly what happened or in what form Satan came to Jesus. Standing on a high mountain (v. 8) would not itself provide a glimpse of 'all the kingdoms of the world'; some supernatural vision is presupposed. Moreover a forty-day fast is scarcely the ideal background for a trek to three separate and rugged sites. When we remember that Paul was not always sure whether his visions were 'in the body or out of the body' (2 Cor. 12:2), we may be cautious about dogmatizing here. But there is no reason to think the framework of the story is purely symbolic as opposed to visionary, representing Jesus' inward struggles; if the demons could address him directly (e.g., 8:20, 31), it is difficult to say Satan wouldn't or couldn't do this." Carson, *Matthew*, 111.

2. Stewart, *Life and Teaching*, 39.

3. Bunyan, *Pilgrim's Progress*, 62.

4. Macleod, *Person of Christ*, 228.

5. Marshall, *Gospel of Luke*, 170–171.

6. "The essential meaning of the incarnation was that Christ took the nature and condition of men and the road to death. In the first temptation, the devil attacked him precisely at this point, tempting him to step out from among the men with whom he has identified in baptism, to use his personal power and authority to mitigate the implications of his humiliation, to refuse the experience of hunger and to end his dependence on ordinary, vulnerable, sources of supply. Significantly, Jesus' answer began with the word 'man': '*Man* does not live on bread alone.' That is what he has become, a man, and he must accept not only the appearance but the reality." Macleod, *Person of Christ*, 227.

7. See Ferguson and Thomas, *Ichthus*, 39–40.

8. Garland, *Luke*, 180.

9. I owe this insight to Sinclair Ferguson who observes that Luke, the traveling companion of Paul, is here presenting the teaching of Paul from Romans 5 and 1 Corinthians 15 in dramatic form. See Ferguson and Thomas, *Ichthus*, 38–42.

10. Adam and Christ "are key, representative figures, heads over contrasting orders of existence. Adam is 'first' (vv. 45, 47), there is no-one before him; Christ is 'second' (v. 47), there is no-one between Adam and him; Christ is 'last' (v. 45), there is no-one after him." Gaffin, "Adam," 4.

11. Irenaeus, *Against Heresies*, 446–448.

12. Herbert, "The Holdfast," *Complete English Poems*, 134.

13. "Jesus has come to gain victory where there has been defeat, to obey where there has been disobedience, to effect justification where there has been condemnation, to bring freedom where there has been bondage, to bring healing where there has been sickness, wholeness where there has been disintegration, reconciliation where there has been alienation, to bring blessing where there has been curse, and life where there has been death.

Where Adam became disobedient by taking and eating, Jesus means to be obedient by taking and by not eating. Only thus can he be 'Adam in reverse' undoing what the First Man did and doing what he failed to do." Ferguson and Thomas, *Ichthus*, 39, 44.

14. "Lo, this day, I see, in our conquering Hero's hand, the grizzly head of the monster sin, all dripping with gouts of gore. Look at it, ye that once were under its tyranny. Look at the terrible lineaments of that hideous and gigantic tyrant. Your Lord has slain your foe. Your sins are dead; he has destroyed them. His own arm, single-handed and alone, has destroyed your gigantic enemy. 'The sting of death is sin, and the strength of sin is the law; but thanks be to God, which giveth us the victory through our Lord Jesus Christ'" Spurgeon, "David's First Victory," 594.

15. John Henry Newman, "Praise to the Holiest in the Height," 1866. Also quoted in Ferguson and Thomas, *Ichthus*, 53.

Chapter 4. With Jesus on the Mountain: Transfiguration

1. Martin, *Abiding Presence*, 25. This is the first book in a thoughtful trilogy on the person and work of Christ; the other two books are. *The Shadow of Calvary* and *The Atonement*.
2. "Behold! Jesus indeed is with you; shining on you; speaking to you—shining forth on you from the biography, resplendent now through the Spirit, with the glory as of the only begotten of the Father; speaking forth to you from the biography, vocal now, through the Spirit, with the Chief Shepherd's voice. . . . [W]e have not the record of a past, but the revelation of a present Saviour." Ibid., 32.
3. This verb is only used four times in the New Testament: in Matthew 17:2, Mark 9:2, 2 Corinthians 3:18, and Romans 12:2.
4. "Both were popularly expected to return to inaugurate the Messianic age, so that their appearance here proclaims Jesus as the Messiah." France, "Matthew," 927.
5. Stewart, *Life and Teaching*, 142.
6. Lewis, *Prince Caspian*, 148–149.
7. Chambers, May 17 entry, *My Utmost for His Highest*.
8. "This glory which we behold, is the glory of the face of God in Jesus Christ . . . or the glorious representation which is made of him in the person of Christ. . . . The glass wherein this glory is represented unto us—proposed unto our view and contemplation—is divine revelation in the Gospel. Herein we behold it, by faith alone." Owen, *Christologia*, 51.
9. Martin describes this as "a revelation without the soul—external to it; and a revelation within the soul itself. There must be outwardly presented to us—'the glory of God in the face of Jesus Christ.' There must be inwardly accomplished in us a work of giving light within. It is from the concurrence of these two revelations that a true knowledge of the Lord—a spiritual perception of his presence and glory—springs.

Glory is presented to the soul: light is made to arise in the soul. The glory is the glory of God as revealed in Jesus Christ: the light is the light of God as conveyed by his Holy Spirit" (*Abiding Presence*, 165).
10. Calvin, "Preface to Olivétan's Translation," 68–70. Consider also these three resources to help you see Christ in all of Scripture: (1) a children's book: Lloyd-Jones, *Jesus Storybook Bible*, (2) a study Bible: *NIV Zondervan Study Bible* features excellent articles on biblical themes and how they point to Christ, and (3) a series of helpful animated videos: The Bible Project (www.jointhebibleproject.com).
11. "This voice was recalling the Church to its unique Teacher Christ, that it might hang on His lips alone." Calvin, *Calvin's New Testament Commentaries*, 2:201.
12. Carmichael, "Divine Paradox," 174.
13. "The word 'dying' or 'mortification' has a different meaning [in 2 Cor. 4:10] than in many other passages of Scripture. For it often means self-denial, by which we renounce the lusts of the flesh and are renewed into obedience to God. Here it means those afflictions that make us meditate on the end of this present life. For the sake of clarity we may call the former meaning internal mortification and the latter external. By both we are conformed to Christ, directly by the one and indirectly by the other." Calvin, *Calvin's New Testament Commentaries*, 10:59.

Chapter 5. With Jesus in the City: Triumphal Entry

1. "The Temple was not simply the 'religious' centre of Israel . . . the equivalent of [the National Cathedral], with [the White House] and [Capitol Hill] being found elsewhere. The Temple combined in itself the functions of all three—religion, national figurehead, and government—and also included what we think of as the City, the financial and economic world [Wall Street]." Wright, *New Testament and the People of God*, 225,

replacing Wright's British examples with the American counterparts he suggests in n. 29. Because of the controversial nature of some of Wright's work, I should note that while his historical work is helpful and thought-provoking on numerous points, I do not always agree with him, especially regarding his view on justification.

2. The details about the colt may also contain an allusion to Genesis 49:10–11, "The scepter shall not depart from Judah, nor the ruler's staff from between his feet, until tribute comes to him; and to him shall be the obedience of the peoples. Binding his foal to the vine and his donkey's colt to the choice vine, he has washed his garments in wine and his vesture in the blood of grapes."

3. Garland, *Luke*, 772.

4. "From about two centuries earlier, palm branches had already become a national (not to say nationalist) symbol. . . . In this instance, it may well have signaled nationalist hope that a messianic liberator was arriving on the scene." Carson, *Gospel According to John*, 432.

5. Stewart, *Life and Teaching*, 146.

6. Lewis, "Necessity of Chivalry," 13.

7. This paragraph compresses into one sentence the outline of the sermon's second point. Edwards, "Excellency of Jesus Christ," 565–571.

8. Ibid., 576–579.

9. Charles Jordan, "Did Christ O'er Sinners Weep," 1875.

10. Hedges, *Christ All Sufficient*, 60–61. As noted then too, I owe this illustration to Tim Keller's sermon "The Openness of the Kingdom," March 19, 2006.

11. Stewart, *Life and Teaching*, 147.

12. Wright, *Jesus and the Victory of God*, 423.

Chapter 6. With Jesus in the Upper Room: Farewell Discourse

1. "We must understand that as long as Christ remains outside of us, and we are separated from him, all that he has suffered and done for the salvation of the human race remains useless and of no value to us." Calvin, *Institutes*, 3.1.1.

2. For a full-length exposition, see Carson, *Farewell Discourse*.

3. For helpful discussion of the Greek term parakletos and its various definitions and connotations, see Carson, *Gospel According to John*, 499.

4. Calvin, *Institutes*, 3.1.1. See also 4.17.33, where Calvin writes that "the secret power of the Spirit is the bond of our union with Christ." Robert Letham agrees, tracing the concept from creation to incarnation, and then to Pentecost: "The Holy Spirit is the One who brings about our union with Christ in our life history" (*Union with Christ*, 52).

5. "The trinitarian union and communion of Father and Son in the Spirit is the analogy for the union and communion between Christ and his people." Ferguson, *Holy Spirit*, 71.

6. Lewis, *Mere Christianity*, 175–176.

7. For more on the relationship of the Spirit to the Father and the Son, see also John 14:26, 15:26; Acts 2:33; Rom. 8:9–10,14–15; and Eph. 1:17.

8. Ferguson, *Holy Spirit*, 71.

9. Owen, *Holy Spirit*, 38–39. For the original version, see Owen, *Pneumatologia*, 199–200.

10. This section is adapted from my article, "What Does It Mean to Abide in Christ?"

11. Calvin, *Calvin's New Testament Commentaries*, 4:96.

12. Owen, "Several Practical Cases," 376–378.

13. These two themes are not the only foci of this prayer, for the prayer's "principle themes include Jesus' obedience to his Father, the glorification of his Father through his death/exaltation, the revelation of God in Christ Jesus, the choosing of the disciples out of

the world, their mission to the world, their unity modeled on the unity of the Father and the Son, and their final destiny in the presence of the Father and the Son." Carson, *Gospel According to John*, 551.

14. Marshall, *Gospel Mystery*, 33–34. See also Bruce H. McRae's modernization of Marshall's book, published by Wipf and Stock in 2005. For details on Marshall's life, see Beeke and Pederson, *Meet the Puritans*, 415–416.

15. "God's Spirit cleanses us by the holiness of Christ and makes us partakers of it. And not by imputation alone, for in that respect He is said to have been made to us righteousness (1 Cor. 1:30); but He is also said to have been made to us sanctification, because He has, so to say, presented us to His Father in his own person . . . that we may be renewed to true holiness by His own Spirit" (Calvin, Calvin's New Testament Commentaries, 4:146). Similarly, "Our sanctification is Christ's sanctification of himself in our humanity progressively applied to and realized in us through the ministry of the Holy Spirit" (Ferguson, *Holy Spirit*, 143).

Chapter 7. With Jesus in the Garden: Gethsemane

1. Warfield, "Emotional Life."
2. "The darkness of Gethsemane must be regarded as but the shadow of Calvary. . . . The sorrows of the garden arose from the prospect and foresight of the sorrows of the cross." Martin, *Shadow of Calvary*, 33.
3. Garland, *Mark*, 539.
4. Ferguson, "Distress of Jesus."
5. Biswas et al., "Curious Case."
6. Warfield, "Emotional Life." See also Jones, *Knowing Christ*, 69–76.
7. Edwards, *Gospel According to Mark*, 440.
8. Wright, *Mark for Everyone*, 199.
9. Knowles, "Grief and Joy," *National Magazine* 8 (October 1905–March 1906): 277. Quoted in Garland, *Mark*, 552.
10. Chalcedonian Creed in Allison, *Historical Theology*, 376.
11. Westminster Confession of Faith, 8.2.
12. Brentnall, *Just a Talker*, 26. He was known as "Rabbi" Duncan because he was such a fine Hebraist and had a deep love for the Jewish people.
13. Lane, *Gospel of Mark*, 516.
14. Martin, *Shadow of Calvary*, 68.
15. I owe these insights to Martin, *Shadow of Calvary*, chapter 6 (see especially pages 127–133).
16. Ferguson, *Holy Spirit*, 37.
17. Elisabeth C. Clephane, "Beneath the Cross of Jesus," 1868. This was also the conclusion of George Herbert's poem, "The Agony" (*Complete English Poems*, 33–34): "Love is that liquor sweet and most divine, / Which my God feels as blood: but I, as wine."

Chapter 8. With Jesus in the Court: Trial

1. Lewis, "God in the Dock," *God in the Dock*, 244.
2. See especially Calvin, *Institutes*, 2.15.1–6, but also Bavinck, *Reformed Dogmatics*, 3:364–369, 475–482, and Owen, *Christologia*, 85–100.
3. Ferguson, *By Grace Alone*, 38.

4. Ibid., 39.

5. Martin, *Shadow of Calvary*, 35. Also, Stewart writes, "We call it a trial; in reality it was an inquisition, and the death sentence, when it was carried out, was nothing more nor less than judicial murder" (*Life and Teaching*, 156).

6. Stott, *Cross of Christ*, 60.

7. Horatius Bonar, "I See the Crowd in Pilate's Hall," 1856. Quoted in part ibid., 60.

8. Ferguson, *By Grace Alone*, 44. See also Ferguson and Thomas, *Ichthus*, 98–100.

9. Calvin, *Institutes*, 2.16.5.

10. Ferguson and Thomas, *Ichthus*, 92.

11. Kelly, *Grounded*, 362.

12. Ferguson and Thomas, *Ichthus*, 93.

13. Martin, *Shadow of Calvary*, 282.

14. What devotional value do Christ's trials have in the life of the believer? This paragraph abridges Hugh Martin's powerful meditations on this question (*Shadow of Calvary*, 294–296).

Chapter 9. With Jesus on the Tree: Crucifixion

1. Quoted in Stott, *Cross of Christ*, 24.

2. Ibid., 68.

3. *Epistle to Diognetus*, 147–148.

4. "The concept of substitution may be said, then, to lie at the heart of both sin and salvation. For the essence of sin is man substituting himself for God, while the essence of salvation is God substituting himself for man. Man asserts himself against God and puts himself where only God deserves to be; God sacrifices himself for man and puts himself where only man deserves to be. Man claims prerogatives that belong to God alone; God accepts penalties which belong to man alone." Stott, *Cross of Christ*, 160.

5. Philip Bliss, "Man of Sorrows," 1875.

6. "Our sins blotted out the sunshine of his Father's face." Stott, *Cross of Christ*, 79.

7. Isaac Watts, "Alas and Did My Savior Bleed," 1707.

8. Brentnall, *Just a Talker*, 26.

9. I've borrowed the phrase "Cross Words" from Paul Wells's excellent book titled *Cross Words*. For two more full-length studies of the cross, see Stott, *Cross of Christ*, and Macleod, *Christ Crucified*.

10. Stott, *Cross of Christ*, 83.

11. Krummacher, *Suffering Savior*, 278–279.

Chapter 10. With Jesus in His Life: Resurrection

1. Updike, "Seven Stanzas at Easter," 20.

2. Bavinck, *Reformed Dogmatics*, 3:436.

3. Wright, *Resurrection of the Son*.

4. Quoted in Warnock, *Raised with Christ*, 34, 54.

5. Wright, *Resurrection of the Son*, 638.

6. Reese, "Save Jesus, Ignore Easter."

7. Wright, *Resurrection of the Son*, 8.

8. Bunyan, *Pilgrim's Progress*, 36.

9. Bavinck, *Reformed Dogmatics*, 3:442.

10. John Wilbur Chapman, "One Day When Heaven Was Filled with His Praises," 1905.

11. Brentnall, *Just a Talker*, 55.

12. Ferguson and Thomas, *Ichthus*, 126.

13. I'm borrowing language from John Donne, C. S. Lewis, and the apostle Paul. See Donne, "Holy Sonnet 10," 313; Lewis, *The Lion, the Witch, and the Wardrobe*, 160; and 1 Corinthians 15:54–57.

14. Lewis, *Miracles*, 237.

15. This is a defining theme in the Reformed theology of Herman Bavinck: "The fundamental theme that shapes Bavinck's entire theology is the trinitarian idea that grace restores nature." Bolt, introduction to Bavinck's *Reformed Dogmatics*, 1:18. See also my sidebar on this theme in chapter 12.

16. Tada, *Heaven*, 51, 53.

17. "The powerful resurrection of Jesus constitutes the sphere within which Christians now live, already justified and reconciled to God, and now looking forward to final rescue from wrath . . . in other words, to the life of the ages to come." Wright, *Resurrection of the Son*, 249.

18. Pippert, *Hope Has Its Reasons*, 125.

19. Charles Wesley, "Christ the Lord is Risen Today," 1739.

Chapter 11. With Jesus in the Heavens: Ascension

1. "Given the place of the ascension in the New Testament (especially the Epistles), it is surprising that it plays a comparatively minor role in the faith and practice of the church. Though affirmed, it does not seem to occupy the same status as Christ's incarnation, death, and resurrection." Horton, *Christian Faith*, 533.

2. Owen, *Christologia*, 235.

3. Ibid., 252.

4. Green, "Salvation," 95.

5. Bavinck, *Reformed Dogmatics*, 3:446.

6. Ibid., 500.

7. The Spirit was, of course, active in the lives of believers under the old covenant, but "The Holy Ghost in this Pentecostal dispensation is what he could not be before: the Spirit of a glorified Saviour" (Brentnall, *Just a Talker*, 96).

8. To further explore these two aspects of salvation, see Murray's *Redemption*, or, for something more contemporary, Peterson's *Salvation Accomplished and Salvation Applied*.

9. Radford, *Collection of Psalms*, 171.

10. Stott, *Baptism and Fullness*, 60.

11. Owen, *Of Communion*, 180.

12. "The ascension is an essential part of Christ's saving accomplishment whereby he brings into God's presence the sacrifice that he made on the cross. . . . Jesus's sacrifice on the cross was finished; nothing could be added to it. But his priestly ministry is bigger than the sacrifice and involves the presentation of his perfect sacrifice in heaven. The ascension is thus the means whereby Christ's ministry of High Priest is brought to its goal. In that sense, Jesus saves by ascending from earth to heaven." Peterson, *Salvation Accomplished*, 177.

13. Charles Wesley, "Arise, My Soul, Arise," 1742.

14. Charitie L. Bancroft, "Before the Throne of God Above," 1863.

15. Dawson, *Jesus Ascended*, 179–180.

16. "We teach that Christ is to be sought by faith, that he may manifest his presence; and the mode of eating which we hold is, that by the gift of his Spirit he transfuses into us the vivifying influence of his flesh." Calvin, "Second Defense," 282.

17. Wallace, *Calvin's Doctrine*, 19, summarizing Calvin, *Institutes*, 4.17.1.

18. Lewis, "The Grand Miracle," *God in the Dock*, 82.

19. Tennyson, Canto 56, *In Memoriam*, 236.

20. Brentnall, *Just a Talker*, 29. Also quoted in Ferguson and Thomas, Ichthus, 140.

21. Christopher Wordsworth, "See, the Conqueror Mounts in Triumph," 1862.

Chapter 12. With Jesus in Glory: Return

1. Bavinck, *Reformed Dogmatics*, 4:689.

2. The doctrine of a pretribulation rapture is a relatively recent development in the history of Christian theology, which is just one among several reasons why I am not persuaded of a pretribulation rapture for the church. As George Ladd notes, "The idea of a secret rapture at a secret coming of Christ had its origin in an 'utterance' in Edward Irving's church, and . . . this was taken to be the voice of the Spirit . . .' It was from that supposed revelation that the modern doctrine . . . arose." See Ladd, *Blessed Hope*, 40–41.

3. Berkhof, *Systematic Theology*, 354.

4. Bavinck, *Reformed Dogmatics*, 4:693–694.

5. Lewis, *Silver Chair*, 211–212.

6. Veith, *Reading Between the Lines*, 143–144.

7. Shakespeare, *Richard III*, V.5.193–195.

8. "Hence arises a wonderful consolation: that we perceive judgment to be in the hands of him who has already destined us to share with him the honor of judging [cf. Matt. 19:28]! Far indeed is he from mounting his judgment seat to condemn us! How could our most merciful Ruler destroy his people? How could the Head scatter his own members? How could our Advocate condemn his clients? For if the apostle dares exclaim that with Christ interceding for us there is no one who can come forth to condemn us [Rom. 8:34, 33], it is much more true, then, that Christ as Intercessor will not condemn those whom he has received into his charge and protection." Calvin, *Institutes*, 2.16.18.

9. John Newton, "Let Us Love and Sing and Wonder," 1774.

10. Bavinck, *Reformed Dogmatics*, 3:577.

11. Bavinck, *De offerande des lofs: overdenkingen voor en na de toelating tot het heilige avondmaal*, quoted in Veenhof, 21. See also Ortlund, "'Created Over a Second Time' or 'Grace Restoring Nature'?"

12. Bavinck, *Reformed Dogmatics*, 4:717.

13. Isaac Watts, "Joy to the World," 1719.

14. I am echoing both Lewis (*Silver Chair*, 202) and Tolkien (*Return of the King*, 246) in this paragraph.

Bibliography

Allison, Gregg R. *Historical Theology: An Introduction to Christian Doctrine.* Grand Rapids, MI: Zondervan, 2011.

Augustine. Sermon 191. In *Sermons 184–229,* translated by Edmund Hill, 42–45. Hyde Park, NY: New City, 1993.

Bavinck, Herman. *Reformed Dogmatics.* Edited by John Bolt. Translated by John Vriend. Vol. 1, *Prolegomena.* Vol. 3, *Sin and Salvation in Christ.* Vol. 4, *Holy Spirit, Church, and New Creation.* Grand Rapids, MI: Baker Academic, 2003–08.

Beeke, Joel R., and Randall J. Pederson. *Meet the Puritans: With a Guide to Modern Reprints.* Grand Rapids, MI: Reformation Heritage, 2006.

Berkhof, Louis. *Systematic Theology.* Grand Rapids, MI: Eerdmans, 1993.

Biswas, Saugato, Trupti Surana, Abhishek De, and Falguni Nag. "A Curious Case of Sweating Blood." *Indian Journal of Dermatology* 58, no. 6 (Nov–Dec 2013): 478–480.

Bock, Darrell L. *Luke 1:1–9:50. Baker Exegetical Commentary on the New Testament.* Grand Rapids, MI: Baker Academic, 1994.

Bowley, J. E. "Pax Romana." In *Dictionary of New Testament Background: A Compendium of Contemporary Biblical Scholarship,* edited by Craig A. Evans and Stanley E. Porter Jr., 771–775. Downers Grove, IL: InterVarsity, 2000.

Brentnall, John M. *"Just a Talker": Sayings of John ("Rabbi") Duncan.* Carlisle, PA: Banner of Truth Trust, 1997.

Bunyan, John. *The Pilgrim's Progress.* Carlisle, PA: Banner of Truth Trust, 1977.

Calvin, John. *Calvin's New Testament Commentaries.* Edited by David W. Torrance and Thomas F. Torrance. Vols. 1–2, *A Harmony of the Gospels Matthew, Mark, and Luke,* translated by A. W. Morrison. Vol. 4, *The Gospel According to St. John 11–21 and the*

First Epistle of John, translated by T. H. L. Parker. Vol. 10, *The Second Epistle of Paul the Apostle to the Corinthians and the Epistles to Timothy*, translated by T. A. Smail. Grand Rapids, MI: Eerdmans, 1994–96.

———. *Institutes of the Christian Religion*. Edited by John T. McNeil. Translated by Ford L. Battles. Philadelphia: Westminster Press, 1960.

———. "Preface to Olivétan's Translation of the New Testament." In *Calvin: Commentaries*, edited and translated by Joseph Haroutunian, 58–73. Philadelphia: Westminster Press, 1958.

———. "Second Defense of the Pious and Orthodox Faith Concerning the Sacraments." In vol. 2, *Tracts and Letters*, edited by Henry Beveridge and Jules Bonnet, translated by Henry Beveridge, 245–345. Carlisle, PA: Banner of Truth Trust, 2009.

Carmichael, Amy. "Divine Paradox." In *Mountain Breezes: The Collected Poems of Amy Carmichael*, 174. Fort Washington, PA: CLC Publications, 1999.

Carson, D. A. *The Farewell Discourse and the Final Prayer of Jesus: An Exposition of John 14–17*. Grand Rapids, MI: Baker, 1988.

———. *The Gospel According to John*. Grand Rapids, MI: Eerdmans, 1991.

———. *Matthew*. In vol. 8, *The Expositor's Bible Commentary*, edited by Frank E. Gaebelein, 1–599. Grand Rapids, MI: Zondervan, 1984.

Carson, R. T. France, J. A. Motyer, and G. J. Wenham, 904–945. Downers Grove, IL: InterVarsity, 1994.

Chambers, Oswald. *My Utmost for His Highest*. Basingstoke, England: Marshall, Morgan, and Scott, 1927.

Cole, Graham A. *He Who Gives Life: The Doctrine of the Holy Spirit*. Wheaton, IL: Crossway, 2007.

Dawson, Gerrit Scott. *Jesus Ascended: The Meaning of Christ's Continuing Incarnation*. Phillipsburg, NJ: P&R, 2004.

Donne, John. "Holy Sonnet 10." In *The Complete English Poems*, 313. New York: Penguin, 1996.

Edwards, James R. *The Gospel According to Mark*. The Pillar New Testament Commentary. Grand Rapids, MI: Eerdmans, 2002.

Edwards, Jonathan. "Dissertation I: Concerning the End for which God Created the World." In *The Works of Jonathan Edwards*, vol. 8, edited by Paul Ramsey, 405–536. New Haven, CT: Yale University Press, 1989.

———. "The Excellency of Jesus Christ." In *The Works of Jonathan Edwards*, vol. 19, edited by M. X. Lesser, 560–594. New Haven, CT: Yale University Press, 2001.

The Epistle to Diognetus. In *The Apostolic Fathers: Early Christian Writings*, edited by Andrew Louth, translated by Maxwell Staniforth. New York: Penguin, 1968.

Ferguson, Sinclair B. *By Grace Alone: How the Grace of God Amazes Me*. Lake Mary, FL: Reformation Trust, 2010.

———. *The Christian Life: A Doctrinal Introduction*. Carlisle, PA: Banner of Truth Trust, 1989.

———. "The Distress of Jesus." Sermon. First Presbyterian Church, Columbia, SC. October 14, 2012.

———. *The Holy Spirit*. Downers Grove, IL: InterVarsity, 1996.

Ferguson, Sinclair B., and Derek W. H. Thomas. *Ichthus: Jesus Christ, God's Son, the Saviour*. Carlisle, PA: Banner of Truth Trust, 2015.

Frame, John M. "Salvation and Theological Pedagogy." Accessed July 13, 2015. http://www.frame-poythress.org/salvation-and-theological-pedagogy.

France, R. T. *The Gospel of Matthew*. The New International Commentary on the New Testament. Grand Rapids, MI: Eerdmans, 2007.

———. "Matthew." In *New Bible Commentary: 21ˢᵗ Century Edition*, edited by D. A.

Gaffin, Richard B. "Adam." In *New Dictionary of Theology*, edited by Sinclair B. Ferguson and David F. Wright, 3–5. Downers Grove, IL: InterVarsity, 1988.

Garland, David E. *Luke. Zondervan Exegetical Commentary on the New Testament*. Grand Rapids, MI: Zondervan, 2011.

———. *Mark. The NIV Application Commentary*. Grand Rapids, MI: Zondervan, 1996.

Gentry, Peter J., and Stephen J. Wellum. *Kingdom through Covenant: A Biblical-Theological Understanding of the Covenants*. Wheaton, IL: Crossway, 2012.

Green, E. Michael. *The Message of Matthew: The Kingdom of Heaven*. Downers Grove, IL: InterVarsity, 2001.

Green, Joel B. "Salvation to the End of the Earth: God as the Saviour in the Acts of the Apostles." In *Witness to the Gospel: The Theology of Acts*, edited by I. Howard Marshall and David Peterson, 83–106. Grand Rapids, MI: Eerdmans, 1998.

Gregory of Nazianzus. "To Cledonius the Priest Against Apollinarius." In vol. 7, *Nicene and Post-Nicene Fathers*, edited by Phillip Schaff and Henry Wace, 439–443. Peabody, MA: Hendrickson, 2004).

Hedges, Brian G. *Christ All Sufficient: An Exposition of Colossians*. Wapwallopen, PA: Shepherd Press, 2016.

———. *Christ Formed in You: The Power of the Gospel for Personal Change*. Wapwallopen, PA: Shepherd Press, 2010.

———. "What Does It Mean to Abide in Christ?" Accessed March 1, 2016. http://www.christianity.com/bible/bible-study/what-does-it-mean-to-abide-in-christ.html.

Herbert, George. *The Complete English Poems*. Edited by John Tobin. New York: Penguin, 2004.

Horton, Michael. *The Christian Faith: A Systematic Theology for Pilgrims on the Way*. Grand Rapids, MI: Zondervan, 2011.

———. *Introducing Covenant Theology*. Grand Rapids, MI: Baker, 2009.

Irenaeus. *Against Heresies*. In vol. 1, *Ante-Nicene Fathers*, edited by Alexander Roberts and James Donaldson, 307–578. Peabody, MA: Hendrickson, 2004.

Jones, Mark. *Knowing Christ*. Carlisle, PA: Banner of Truth Trust, 2015.

Kelly, Douglas F. *Grounded in Holy Scripture and Understood in the Light of the Church*. Vol. 1 of *Systematic Theology*. Ross-shire, Scotland: Christian Focus, 2014.

Krummacher, F. W. *The Suffering Savior*. Chicago, IL: Moody, 1966.

Ladd, George E. *The Blessed Hope: A Biblical Study of the Second Advent and the Rapture*. Grand Rapids, MI: Eerdmans, 1956.

Lane, William L. *The Gospel of Mark*. The New International Commentary on the New Testament. Grand Rapids, MI: Eerdmans, 1974.

Letham, Robert. *Union with Christ: In Scripture, History, and Theology*. Phillipsburg, NJ: P&R, 2011.

Lewis, C. S. *God in the Dock: Essays on Theology and Ethics*. Grand Rapids, MI: Eerdmans, 1970.

———. *The Lion, the Witch, and the Wardrobe*. New York: Collier, 1970.

———. *Mere Christianity*. New York, NY: HarperOne, 1980.

———. *Miracles: A Preliminary Study*. New York: HarperCollins, 2001.

———. "The Necessity of Chivalry." In *Present Concerns: Essays by C. S. Lewis*, edited by Walter Hooper, 13–16. New York: Harcourt, 1986.

———. *Prince Caspian*. New York: Collier, 1970.

———. *The Silver Chair*. New York: Collier, 1970.

Lloyd-Jones, Sally. *The Jesus Storybook Bible: Every Story Whispers His Name*. Grand Rapids, MI: Zonderkids, 2007.

Macleod, Donald. *Christ Crucified: Understanding the Atonement*. Downers Grove, IL: InterVarsity, 2014.

———. *The Person of Christ*. Downers Grove, IL: InterVarsity, 1998.

Marshall, I. Howard. *The Gospel of Luke*. The New International Greek Testament Commentary. Grand Rapids, MI: Eerdmans, 1978.

Marshall, Walter. *The Gospel Mystery of Sanctification: Growing in Holiness by Living in Union with Christ*. Welwyn, England: Evangelical Press, 1981.

Martin, Hugh. *The Abiding Presence*. Ross-shire, Scotland: Christian Focus, 2009.

———. *The Atonement: In Its Relations to the Covenant, the Priesthood, the Intercession of Our Lord*. Carlisle, PA: Banner of Truth Trust, 2013.

———. *Christ for Us: Sermons of Hugh Martin*. Carlisle, PA: Banner of Truth Trust, 1998.

———. *The Shadow of Calvary: Gethsemane, the Arrest, the Trial*. Carlisle, PA: Banner of Truth Trust, 1983.

Murray, John. *Redemption: Accomplished and Applied*. Grand Rapids, MI: Eerdmans, 1955.

The NIV Zondervan Study Bible: Built on the Truth of Scripture and Centered on the Gospel Message. Edited by D. A. Carson. Grand Rapids, MI: Zondervan, 2015.

Ortlund, Dane C. "Created Over a Second Time" or "Grace Restoring Nature"? Edwards and Bavinck on the Heart of Christian Salvation." *The Bavinck Review* 3 (2012): 9–29. Accessed March 18, 2016. https://bavinckinstitute.org/wp-content/uploads/2012/06/TBR3a-Ortlund1.pdf.

Osborne, Grant R. *Matthew*. Zondervan Exegetical Commentary on the New Testament. Grand Rapids, MI: Zondervan, 2010.

Owen, John. *Christologia: A Declaration of the Glorious Mystery of the Person of Christ*. In vol. 1, *The Works of John Owen*, edited by William H. Goold, 1–272. Carlisle, PA: Banner of Truth Trust, 1965.

———. *The Holy Spirit: The Treasures of John Owen for Today's Readers*. Abridged by R. J. K. Law. Carlisle, PA: Banner of Truth Trust, 1998.

———. *Meditations and Discourses on the Glory of Christ*. In vol. 1, *The Works of John Owen*, edited by William H. Goold, 274–417. Carlisle, PA: Banner of Truth Trust, 1965.

———. *Of Communion with God the Father, Son, and Holy Ghost*. In vol. 2, *The Works of John Owen*, edited by William H. Goold, 2–274. Carlisle, PA: Banner of Truth Trust, 1965.

———. *Pneumatologia*. Vol. 3, *The Works of John Owen*, edited by William H. Goold. Carlisle, PA: Banner of Truth Trust, 1965.

———. "Several Practical Cases of Conscience Resolved." In vol. 9, *The Works of John Owen*, edited by William H. Goold, 358–408. Carlisle, PA: Banner of Truth Trust, 1965.

Peterson, Robert A. *Salvation Accomplished by the Son: The Work of Christ*. Wheaton, IL: Crossway, 2012.

———. *Salvation Applied by the Spirit: Union with Christ*. Wheaton, IL: Crossway, 2014.

Pippert, Rebecca Manley. *Hope Has Its Reasons: The Search to Satisfy Our Deepest Longings*. Downers Grove, IL: InterVarsity, 2001.

Plantinga, Cornelius, Jr. *Not the Way It's Supposed to Be: A Breviary on Sin*. Grand Rapids, MI: Eerdmans, 1995.

Radford, Joseph. *A Collection of Psalms and Hymns for Public Worship*. London: J. Chalmers, 1790.

Reese, Erik. "Save Jesus, Ignore Easter." Accessed February 27, 2015. http://www.faithstreet.com/onfaith/2009/04/03/save-jesus-ignore-easter/3758.

Shakespeare, William. *The Tragedy of Richard the Third*. Oxford, England: Oxford University Press, 2000.

Smith, Z. G. "Gospel Genre." In *The Lexham Bible Dictionary*, edited by John D. Barry. Bellingham. WA: Lexham, 2014. Logos Bible Software.

Spurgeon, C. H. "David's First Victory." In vol. 50, *The Metropolitan Tabernacle Pulpit Sermons*, 589–600. London: Passmore & Alabaster, 1901.

Stapert, Calvin R. *Handel's Messiah: Comfort for God's People*. Grand Rapids, MI: Eerdmans, 2010.

Stewart, James S. *The Life and Teaching of Jesus Christ*. New York: Abingdon, 2000.

Stott, John R. W. *Baptism and Fullness: The Work of the Holy Spirit Today*. Downers Grove, IL: InterVarsity, 2006.

———. *The Cross of Christ*. Downers Grove, IL: InterVarsity, 1986.

Tada, Joni Eareckson. *Heaven: Your Real Home*. Grand Rapids, MI: Zondervan, 1997.

Tennyson, Alfred. *In Memoriam A.H.H.* In *The Major Works*, edited by Adam Roberts, 203–292. New York: Oxford University Press, 2009.

Tolkien, J. R. R. *The Children of Hurin*. Boston: Houghton Mifflin Harcourt, 2007.

———. *The Return of the King*. New York: Del Rey Books, 1966.

———. *The Two Towers*. Boston: Houghton Mifflin, 1966.

Updike, John. "Seven Stanzas at Easter." In *Collected Poems: 1953–1993*, 20–21. New York: Knopf, 1993.

Veenhof, Jan. *Nature and Grace in Herman Bavinck*. Translated by Albert M. Wolters. Sioux Center, IA: Dordt College Press, 2006.

Veith, Gene Edward, Jr. *Reading Between the Lines: A Christian Guide to Literature*. Wheaton, IL: Crossway, 1990.

Wallace, Ronald S. *Calvin's Doctrine of the Christian Life*. Eugene, OR: Wipf and Stock, 1997.

Warfield, B. B. "The Emotional Life of Our Lord." In *The Person and Work of Christ*, 93–145. Phillipsburg, NJ: P&R, 1950. Accessed March 11, 2016. https://www.monergism.com/thethreshold/articles/onsite/emotionallife.html.

Warnock, Adrian. *Raised with Christ: How the Resurrection Changes Everything*. Wheaton, IL: Crossway, 2009.

Wells, Paul. *Cross Words: The Biblical Doctrine of the Atonement*. Ross-shire, Scotland: Christian Focus, 2005.

Williamson, Paul R. *Sealed with an Oath: Covenant in God's Unfolding Purpose*. Downers Grove, IL: IVP Academic, 2007.

Wright, N. T. *Jesus and the Victory of God*. Minneapolis, MN: Fortress, 1997.

———. *Mark for Everyone*. Louisville, KY: Westminster John Knox, 2004.

———. *The New Testament and the People of God*. Minneapolis, MN: Fortress, 1992.

———. *The Resurrection of the Son of God*. Minneapolis, MN: Fortress, 2003.

Subject Index

Scripture Index

Acknowledgments

Publishing a book is sort of like growing a garden. A partial list of necessary components: soil, seeds, water and sunlight, fertilizer, trellises for tender plants, someone to pull weeds, lots of patience, and someone to harvest the fruit.

If my mind was the soil, it was tilled, cultivated, and prepared by many mentors and friends. I'm particularly grateful for my parents and their steadfast trust in Christ. I first heard the gospel from them.

The seeds for this book were numerous, but I owe the seminal ideas especially to Hugh Martin's book *The Abiding Presence* and Sinclair Ferguson's sermons on the life of Christ (now published in his book *Ichthus: Jesus Christ, God's Son, the Savior,* co-authored with Derek Thomas).

My church family provided the water and sunlight that helped this material grow into book form. *With Jesus* originated in an Elders retreat in 2014, then developed into a sermon series, and finally into this book. I'm grateful for the elders and members who continue to provide generous time for writing.

Fertilizer came in the form of further research in 2016 (some, but not all, of which is reflected in the notes). In addition to Ferguson and Martin, I'm grateful to the following authors, who have helped clarify and sharpen my Christology and understanding of union with Christ: Michael Horton, D. A. Carson, Mark Jones, Derek Thomas, Donald Macleod, Robert Letham, B. B. Warfield, Herman Bavinck, Walter Marshall, John Owen, John Calvin, and Irenaeus of Lyons.

Shepherd Press provided the trellis, while my editor, Jennifer Strange, not only pulled the weeds, but helped the fruit of my research ripen and mature.

Everyone involved has exercised patience with me in a variety of ways, but none so much as my beautiful wife and children.

You, kind reader, get to harvest the fruit. I hope you find it both tasteful and nourishing.

Of all my books, this one is my favorite, so it is only fitting that I dedicate to my favorite person. Holly, this one is for you

Other Books by Brian G. Hedges

Connect with Brian Hedges

Read more at Brian's blog:
www.brianghedges.com

Sermons: www.fulkersonpark.com/audio

 @brianghedges

 www.facebook.com/brian.g.hedges

www. shepherdpress.com